PRESIDENT OBAMA

HERO OR VILLAIN

OF

CAPITALISM?

If you vote for the re-election of President Obama you have done the following things, you have trust in the skills and future of American workers; you have helped to preserve the dreams of the middle class, the future of the coming generation, education and healthcare of all Americans that share in the dreams of Andrew Jackson, believe me, you have made America a better place for all to live no matter the color, sex or religion or none of it. ORACLE

ALSO BY ZENTS SOWUNMI

(ALSO KNOWN AS ORACLE)

PRESIDENT OBAMA

HERO OR VILLAIN

OF

CAPITALISM?

ECONOMIC WARS AND WORDS

BY

ZENTS K. SOWUNMI

(ALSO KNOWN AS ORACLE)

For additional copies of this or other Zents Sowunmi titles write to:

Korloki Publishing Company (A subsidiary of Allzents Groups Inc.)

P.O. Box 300605 Brooklyn New York 11230 USA.

Please allow 4 to 6 weeks for delivery order thru. kpcbooks@yahoo.com.

20 REASONS WHY

PRESIDENT OBAMA

May win this election,

Including his ECONOMIC
WARS AND WORDS

Cover design by: Sel P Inc.

Interior design: Sel P Inc.

Photo: President Barack Obama ref: www.thegoldsteinstandard.com

Credit: Goldstein Communications

Summary: Power, Politics and People in America.

ISBN: 13   978-1936739080

     10   1936739089

PRINTED IN USA

DEDICATION

This book is dedicated to
the dreams

Of middle class of

American society

PRESIDENT OBAMA

HERO OR VILLAIN

OF

CAPITALISM?

FOREWORD

Most of us are either too busy, too lazy, don't have the time, or just don't care to research and collect all the facts and statistics about a certain issue. We tend to believe what is said, go with the status quo, and take what's reported by some at face value even when it is a lie.

I have known Zents Sowunmi for 15 years and one thing I have always admired about him is his tenacity in reading, researching and gathering facts and presenting those facts in a conversation held with him or through one of the many articles he has written.

To some people truth is a hard pill to swallow. And, despite facts, they remain in denial of certain truths. However, the most widely read book in the world, the Bible says, *ye shall know the truth and the truth shall set you free.* Truth is defined by Webster's dictionary as—*something that has been proven by facts or sincerity.* Lie is defined as—*a false statement made with deliberate intent to deceive; an intentional untruth; a falsehood.* It is our choice to believe the truth or believe a lie.

Like a beneficiary inherits land, property, and assets from their ancestor, in the pages of **OBAMA: THE HERO or VILLAIN OF CAPITALISM** you will read and discover the facts and truth about the system and conditions President Obama inherited from the Presidents before him, more importantly, the President immediately before him, George Bush. Truth is absolute! It will always remain.

As an inheritor of problems and out of control conditions, did President Obama handle things to the best of his ability considering what was handed over to him? You be the judge! As Shakespeare said, *This Above All: To Thy Own Self Be True!* Now we are equipped with the *proven facts* to vote in all fairness and good consciousness, and not just based on myths, fairy tales and lies! Shakespeare went on to say in the same verse: *Thou canst not then be false to any man.*

See you at the poles in the November 2012 election.

Della Faye
Author, Speaker, Performance Improvement Trainer

APPRECIATION

I'd like to thank my Editor Kola Bello and his charming wife Bunmi for their suggestions and diligence to go through the documents in the course of editing this book which came out of my online writings in the last four years, and several thousands of my online readers; like George Harvey, Linda, Marie, Jon Kay, Dr. Adeyemi, Ahmed Na'abba, Makun, Falayajo Jr. Demetras, Kathy Jenkins–Ewa, Jacqueline Vasquez, Dauda Shokeye, Lillian Lockhart, Jacqueline Jacci Johnson, Tunde Akogun, Cxavier Noges, Dayo Bell, Dr. Dahiru, Madam Ms. John, Davis, Judy Lambert, Ginny Cole, Joyce Quasesseva, Frank Solomon, Flossie Espendza, Clement Oni, Mary Smith and my dear "Moin Paduruga" Elena and others that could not be mentioned, they all inspired me to keep on writing even though we sometimes don't agree on some issues, however, it never affected my respect for their opinions and contributions to mine on some national and international issues.

I also want to show my appreciation to the people of Brooklyn New York particularly my Jewish Community on Coney Island Avenue and the staff of Brooklyn Center For Rehab for allowing me to enjoy what it takes to be a New

Yorker after 14 years in Texas, the change of environment could be challenging and very interesting.

I also want to thank my mother, Hannah for the love she gave me, my two children Stella and Peter in Texas, a state we now called home, my son in-law Femi and lots of lifelong friends I made in Texas, my new friends in New York and group of writers and unending fun loving people of New York, a City that operates 24 hours.

Finally, I will like to acknowledge the support of Della Faye in most of my ventures and writings and to thank her for believing in me like I do with her.

However, any mistake in this book is entirely on my responsibility.

Zents Sowunmi
August 10, 2012

Preface

This book is not intended to be a work of biased analysis of American economy but a presentation of material facts based on the promises of President Obama before he took oath as President of the United States of America in his inaugural speech and his 2009 State of the Union address, which tried to undo almost impossible tasks from the mess left behind by the past administration of President George Bush which was moving toward the end of Capitalism in 2008.

President Andrew Jackson a Democrat, one of the founders of the Party somehow included in the policies of the party to take care of the sick, the poor, women and children, to hate debt and level the ground for all Americans, which has been the foundation of what the Democrats stand for which is to protect the middle class Americans.

The policy of "trickle down" of President Reagan and President George Bush Tax policy introduced earlier made a complete fool of the working class all which may seem impossible to be effective in the 21st Century if the United States of America still wants to compete with other nations, economically, and politically, in a world with dynamic cyberspace changes which will require the greatest nation on earth to retool and rebuild.

Zents Sowunmi
(ORACLE)

PRESIDENT OBAMA

HERO OR VILLAIN

OF

CAPITALISM?

ECONOMIC WARS AND WORDS

BY

ZENTS K. SOWUNMI

TABLE OF CONTENTS

INTRODUCTION

It is better to look at the promises of President Obama in the last four years, his commitment in his own words from his acceptance speech in the state of Illinois, his inaugural speech, and of his State of the Union address, and it will help to understand the type of leadership President Barack Obama is to the United States of America.

What will be the legacy of this presidency in the next decade, in his own words and the economic wars the nation is facing, the reason why he should or should not be re-elected President of the United States of America, the effect of his re-election or not, on the country particularly on the middle class.

This book will assist you to make the decision that will help change the society and commitment of keeping the dreams of the middle class.

Thank you.

Zents Sowunmi
August 10, 2012

"We are the first nation to be founded for the sake of an idea—the idea that each of us deserves the chance to shape our own destiny. That's why centuries of pioneers and immigrants have risked everything to come here...The future is ours to win. But to get there, we cannot stand still."

-President Barack Obama

ONE

ʊʊʊʊʊʊʊʊʊ

WHAT PRESIDENT CLINTON LEFT BEHIND?

By the time President Bill Clinton left office in the year 2001, he had made landmark achievements that would be difficult to match in the history of America for any President in American history. Clinton created over twenty two million new jobs; he committed himself to paying off the national debt first created by the doyen of the Republican Party; late President Ronald Reagan whose first three trillion dollars debt negotiation terms and payback remained ambiguous to the people.

President George Bush senior, who succeeded Ronald Reagan, bloated the national debt to eight trillion dollars while

President Clinton who defeated him in 1992 during his second term bid increased the taxes, and thereby reduced the debt to five trillion dollars.

President Clinton warned the nation to take care of social security, Medicare, and Medicaid, balanced budget and plan for the baby boomers that may affect the 21st Century America. He was convinced that if the country continued on the right path and build on the laid down policies of his eight - year administration the country would be debt free in the next decade.

Unfortunately, the hope of the Liberals and Independents that Vice President Al Gore would succeed President Clinton was dashed by the outcome of Florida delegates' election result which turned out in favor of Governor Bush of Texas. A State, he had his brother as the Governor and a biased Secretary of State who was elected into the House of Congress two years later by the Republican Party.

The Supreme Court, which was a conservative dominated group of nine, voted on ideological level of 5 against 4 and a President George Bush Jr. with different ideology and policies took the nation on a different route or direction? His policies were a complete difference from the middle class oriented policies of President Bill Clinton.

Some gains of President Clinton policies on the economy had little impact during the eight years of President Bush leadership. The Tax policies translated to Tax benefit that was enjoyed mostly by the top one percent rich in the society. The outcome of this policy affected the treasury department; it had insufficient resources to run the government, in addition to funding two active wars and many military locations all over the world.

The robust Middle Class - the dreams and aspirations of most Americans, was thus threatened.

America's economic growth and international competitiveness depend on our ability to innovate. President Obama believes that we will create the jobs and industries of the future and restore middle class security by doing what America does best – investing in the creativity and imagination of our people. We must out-innovate, out-educate, and out-build the rest of the world to ensure that our nation achieves rapid, sustained and broad-based economic growth

White House press release

TWO

ꭥꭥꭥꭥꭥꭥꭥꭥꭥ

THE MESSY ECONOMY OF PRESIDENT GEORGE BUSH

The tail end of President George Bush presidency was more than a mess as it was almost the end of Capitalism in America. The nation witnessed depression in the economy which resulted in capital flight, collapse of housing market, distress in banking, auto industries, and financial sectors where life savings and investments vanished. It as was rightly described in the movie by James Douglas, "Wall Street" everything went into the thin air.

Those who thought that they had their future already secured, had to go back to work, even at the age of seventy. There were massive lay off of workers not just in hundreds but a figure very close to a million every month.

The few surviving banks in the country, did not entertain further credit facilities. Many people walked away from everything that was dear to them, including families and properties. It was the fear of the loss that drove the system down more than the near collapse of the economy. The era of capital flight was overwhelming both in the private and public sectors of the economy.

It was the beginning of bailouts system and the hopes of the nation's survival was hinged on the President elect - Barack Obama, for direction and comfort rather than the incumbent president. At a time, those who had supported Senator Hillary Clinton during the Democrats primaries started doubting the President elect capability to fix the economy. They had thought the new President, would seek the advice of the former President Bill Clinton.

Whereas, most of the President economic advisers were from Clinton's administration and his colleagues from Harvard University and Nobel Award winners, it was the hope of the nation that the magic wand of the robust period of President Clinton would be re-activated again.

If demography is destiny, population movements are the motor of history."

Samuel P Huntington

THREE

ℼℼℼℼℼℼℼℼℼ

OBAMA: HIS WARS, WORDS AND PROMISES

It will be okay to just read again, what President Obama said, when he was declared the winner of the 2008 election, his acceptance including his inaugural speech to understand why and how he faced all the challenges given to him in his first term as president of the United States of America. (Ref White House)

President Elect acceptance speech

Complete Text of Remarks by President-Elect Barack Obama, Nov. 4, 2008, Chicago, Ill.

If there is anyone out there who still doubts that America is a place where all things are possible; who still wonders if the dream of our founders is alive in our time; who still questions the power of our democracy, tonight is your answer.

It's the answer told by lines that stretched around schools and churches in numbers this nation has never seen; by people who waited three hours and four hours, many for the very first time in their lives, because they believed that this time must be different; that their voice could be that difference.

It's the answer spoken by young and old, rich and poor, Democrat and Republican, black, white, Latino, Asian, Native American, gay, straight, disabled and not disabled - Americans who sent a message to the world that we have never been a collection of red states and blue states: we are, and always will be, the United States of America.

It's the answer that led those who have been told for so long by so many to be cynical, and fearful, and doubtful of what we can achieve to put their hands on the arc of history and bend it once more toward the hope of a better day.

It's been a long time coming, but tonight, because of what we did on this day, in this election, at this defining moment, change has come to America.

I just received a very gracious call from Sen. McCain. He fought long and hard in this campaign, and he's fought even longer and harder for the country he loves. He has endured sacrifices for America that most of us cannot begin to imagine, and we are better off for the service rendered by this brave and selfless leader. I congratulate him and Gov. Palin for all they have achieved, and I look forward to working with them to renew this nation's promise in the months ahead.

I want to thank my partner in this journey, a man who campaigned from his heart and spoke for the men and women he grew up with on the streets of Scranton and rode with on that train home to Delaware, the vice president-elect of the United States, Joe Biden.

I would not be standing here tonight without the unyielding support of my best friend for the last sixteen years, the rock of our family and the love of my life, our nation's next First Lady, Michelle Obama. Sasha and Malia, I love you both so much, and you have earned the new puppy that's coming with us to the White House. And while she's no longer with us, I know my grandmother is watching, along with the family that made me who I am. I miss them tonight, and know that my debt to them is beyond measure.

To my campaign manager David Plouffe, my chief strategist David Axelrod, and the best campaign team ever assembled in the history of politics – you made this happen, and I am forever grateful for what you've sacrificed to get it done.

But above all, I will never forget who this victory truly belongs to –- it belongs to you.

I was never the likeliest candidate for this office. We didn't start with much money or many endorsements. Our campaign was not hatched in the halls of Washington –- it began in the backyards of Des Moines and the living rooms of Concord and the front porches of Charleston.

It was built by working men and women who dug into what little savings they had to give five dollars and ten dollars and twenty dollars to this cause. It grew strength from the young people who rejected the myth of their generation's apathy; who left their homes and their families for jobs that offered little pay and less sleep; from the not-so-young people who braved the bitter cold and scorching heat to knock on the doors of perfect strangers; from the millions of Americans who volunteered, and organized, and proved that more than two centuries later, a government of the people, by the people and for the people has not perished from this Earth. This is your victory.

I know you didn't do this just to win an election and I know you didn't do it for me. You did it because you understand the enormity of the task that lies ahead. For even as we celebrate tonight, we know the challenges that tomorrow will bring are the greatest of our lifetime –– two wars, a planet in peril, the worst financial crisis in a century.

Even as we stand here tonight, we know there are brave Americans waking up in the deserts of Iraq and the mountains of Afghanistan to risk their lives for us. There are mothers and fathers who will lie awake after their children fall asleep and wonder how they'll make the mortgage, or pay their doctor's bills, or save enough for college. There is new energy to harness and new jobs to be created; new schools to build and threats to meet and alliances to repair.

The road ahead will be long. Our climb will be steep. We may not get there in one year or even one term, but America –- I have never been more hopeful than I am tonight that we will get there. I promise you –- we as a people will get there.

There will be setbacks and false starts. There are many who won't agree with every decision or policy I make as president, and we know that government can't solve every problem. But I will always be honest with you about the challenges we face.

I will listen to you, especially when we disagree. And above all, I will ask you join in the work of remaking this nation the only way it's been done in America for 221 years block by block, brick by brick, calloused hand by calloused hand.

What began twenty-one months ago in the depths of winter must not end on this autumn night. This victory alone is not the change we seek -— it is only the chance for us to make that change. And that cannot happen if we go back to the way things were. It cannot happen without you.

So let us summon a new spirit of patriotism; of service and responsibility where each of us resolves to pitch in and work harder and look after not only ourselves, but each other. Let us remember that if this financial crisis taught us anything, it's that we cannot have a thriving Wall Street while Main Street suffers - in this country, we rise or fall as one nation; as one people.

Let us resist the temptation to fall back on the same partisanship and pettiness and immaturity that have poisoned our politics for so long. Let us remember that it was a man from this state who first carried the banner of the Republican Party to the White House –- a party founded on the values of self-reliance, individual liberty, and national unity.

Those are values we all share, and while the Democratic Party has won a great victory tonight, we do so with a measure of humility and determination to heal the divides that have held back our progress. As Lincoln said to a nation far more divided than ours, "We are not enemies, but friends...though passion may have strained it must not break our bonds of affection." And to those Americans whose support I have yet to earn -– I may not have won your vote, but I hear your voices, I need your help, and I will be your president too.

And to all those watching tonight from beyond our shores, from parliaments and palaces to those who are huddled around radios in the forgotten corners of our world –-

our stories are singular, but our destiny is shared, and a new dawn of American leadership is at hand. To those who would tear this world down –- we will defeat you.

To those who seek peace and security –- we support you. And to all those who have wondered if America's beacon still burns as bright –- tonight we proved once more that the true strength of our nation comes not from our the might of our arms or the scale of our wealth, but from the enduring power of our ideals: democracy, liberty, opportunity, and unyielding hope.

For that is the true genius of America - that America can change? Our union can be perfected. And what we have already achieved gives us hope for what we can and must achieve tomorrow.

This election had many firsts and many stories that will be told for generations. But one that's on my mind tonight is about a woman who cast her ballot in Atlanta. She's a lot like the millions of others who stood in line to make their voice heard in this election except for one thing Ann Nixon Cooper is 106 years old.

She was born just a generation past slavery; a time when there were no cars on the road or planes in the sky; when someone like her couldn't vote for two reasons - because she was a woman and because of the color of her skin.

And tonight, I think about all that she's seen throughout her century in America –- the heartache and the hope; the struggle and the progress; the times we were told that we can't, and the people who pressed on with that American creed: Yes, we can.

At a time when women's voices were silenced and their hopes dismissed, she lived to see them stand up and speak out and reach for the ballot. Yes, we can.

When there was despair in the Dust Bowl and depression across the land, she saw a nation conquer fear itself with a New Deal, new jobs and a new sense of common purpose. Yes, we can.

When the bombs fell on our harbor and tyranny threatened the world, she was there to witness a generation rise to greatness and a democracy was saved. Yes, we can.

She was there for the buses in Montgomery, the hoses in Birmingham, a bridge in Selma, and a preacher from Atlanta who told a people that "We Shall Overcome." Yes, we can.

A man touched down on the moon, a wall came down in Berlin, and a world was connected by our own science and imagination. And this year, in this election, she touched her finger to a screen, and cast her vote, because after 106 years in America, through the best of times and the darkest of hours, she knows how America can change. Yes, we can.

America, we have come so far. We have seen so much. But there is so much more to do. So tonight, let us ask ourselves –- if our children should live to see the next century; if my daughters should be so lucky to live as long as Ann Nixon Cooper, what change will they see? What progress will we have made?

This is our chance to answer that call. This is our moment. This is our time –- to put our people back to work and open doors of opportunity for our kids; to restore prosperity and promote the cause of peace; to reclaim the American Dream and reaffirm that fundamental truth –- that out of many, we are one; that while we breathe, we hope, and where we are met with cynicism, and doubt, and those who tell us that we can't, we will respond with that timeless creed that sums up the spirit of a people:

Yes, we can. Thank you, God bless you, and may God bless the United States of America

Inaugural speech of Barack Obama

PRESIDENT BARACK OBAMA: Thank you. Thank you.

CROWD: Obama! Obama! Obama! Obama!

My fellow citizens: I stand here today humbled by the task before us, grateful for the trust you have bestowed, mindful of the sacrifices borne by our ancestors.

I thank President Bush for his service to our nation as well as the generosity and cooperation he has shown throughout this transition.

Forty-four Americans have now taken the presidential oath.

The words have been spoken during rising tides of prosperity and the still waters of peace. Yet, every so often the oath is taken amidst gathering clouds and raging storms. At these moments, America has carried on not simply because of the skill or vision of those in high office, but because we the People have remained faithful to the ideals of our forebears, and true to our founding documents.

So it has been. So it must be with this generation of Americans.

That we are in the midst of crisis is now well understood. Our nation is at war against a far-reaching network of violence and hatred. Our economy is badly weakened, a consequence of greed and irresponsibility on the part of some but also our collective failure to make hard choices and prepare the nation for a new age.

Homes have been lost, jobs shed, businesses shuttered. Our health care is too costly, our schools fail too many, and each day brings further evidence that the ways we use energy strengthen our adversaries and threaten our planet.

These are the indicators of crisis, subject to data and statistics. Less measurable, but no less profound, is a sapping of confidence across our land; a nagging fear that America's decline is inevitable, that the next generation must lower its sights.

Today I say to you that the challenges we face are real, they are serious and they are many. They will not be met easily or in a short span of time. But know this America: They will be met.

(APPLAUSE)

On this day, we gather because we have chosen hope over fear, unity of purpose over conflict and discord.

On this day, we come to proclaim an end to the petty grievances and false promises, the recriminations and worn-out dogmas that for far too long have strangled our politics.

We remain a young nation, but in the words of Scripture, the time has come to set aside childish things. The time has come to reaffirm our enduring spirit; to choose our better history; to carry forward that precious gift, that noble idea, passed on from generation to generation: the God-given promise that all are equal, all are free, and all deserve a chance to pursue their full measure of happiness.

(APPLAUSE)

In reaffirming the greatness of our nation, we understand that greatness is never a given. It must be earned. Our journey has never been one of shortcuts or settling for less.

It has not been the path for the faint-hearted, for those who prefer leisure over work, or seek only the pleasures of riches and fame.

Rather, it has been the risk-takers, the doers, the makers of things -- some celebrated, but more often men and women obscure in their labor -- which have carried us up the long, rugged path towards prosperity and freedom.

For us, they packed up their few worldly possessions and traveled across oceans in search of a new life. For us, they toiled in sweatshops and settled the West, endured the lash of the whip and plowed the hard earth.

For us, they fought and died in places Concord and Gettysburg; Normandy and Khe Sanh.

Time and again these men and women struggled and sacrificed and worked till their hands were raw so that we might live a better life. They saw America as bigger than the sum of our individual ambitions as; greater than all the differences of birth or wealth or faction.

This is the journey we continue today. We remain the most prosperous, powerful nation on Earth. Our workers are no less productive than when this crisis began. Our minds are no less inventive, our goods and services no less needed than they were last week or last month or last year. Our capacity remains undiminished. But our time of standing pat, of protecting narrow interests and putting off unpleasant decisions -- that time has surely passed.

Starting today, we must pick ourselves up, dust ourselves off, and begin again the work of remaking America.

(APPLAUSE)

For everywhere we look, there is work to be done.

The state of our economy calls for action: bold and swift. And we will act not only to create new jobs but to lay a new foundation for growth.

We will build the roads and bridges, the electric grids and digital lines that feed our commerce and bind us together.

We will restore science to its rightful place and wield technology's wonders to raise health care's quality...

(APPLAUSE)

... And lower its costs.

We will harness the sun and the winds and the soil to fuel our cars and run our factories. And we will transform our schools and colleges and universities to meet the demands of a new age.

All this we can do. All this we will do.

Now, there are some who question the scale of our ambitions, who suggest that our system cannot tolerate too many big plans. Their memories are short, for they have forgotten what this country has already done, what free men and women can achieve when imagination is joined to common purpose and necessity to courage.

What the cynics fail to understand is that the ground has shifted beneath them, that the stale political arguments that have consumed us for so long, no longer apply.

MR. The question we ask today is not whether our government is too big or too small, but whether it works, whether it helps families find jobs at a decent wage, care they can afford, a retirement that is dignified.

Where the answer is yes, we intend to move forward. Where the answer is no, programs will end.

And those of us who manage the public's dollars will be held to account, to spend wisely, reform bad habits, and do our business in the light of day, because only then can we restore the vital trust between a people and their government.

Nor is the question before us whether the market is a force for good or ill. Its power to generate wealth and expand freedom is unmatched.

But this crisis has reminded us that without a watchful eye, the market can spin out of control. The nation cannot prosper long when it favors only the prosperous.

The success of our economy has always depended not just on the size of our gross domestic product, but on the reach of our prosperity; on the ability to extend opportunity to every willing heart -- not out of charity, but because it is the surest route to our common good.

(APPLAUSE)

As for our common defense, we reject as false the choice between our safety and our ideals.

Our founding fathers faced with perils that we can scarcely imagine, drafted a charter to assure the rule of law and the rights of man, a charter expanded by the blood of generations.

Those ideals still light the world, and we will not give them up for expedience's sake.

And so, to all other peoples and governments who are watching today, from the grandest capitals to the small village where my father was born: know that America is a friend of each nation and every man, woman and child who seeks a future of peace and dignity, and we are ready to lead once more.

(APPLAUSE)

Recall that earlier generations faced down fascism and communism not just with missiles and tanks, but with the sturdy alliances and enduring convictions.

They understood that our power alone cannot protect us, nor does it entitle us to do as we please. Instead, they knew that our power grows through its prudent use. Our security emanates from the justness of our cause; the force of our example; the tempering qualities of humility and restraint.

We are the keepers of this legacy, guided by these principles once more; we can meet those new threats that demand even greater effort, even greater cooperation and understanding between nations. We'll begin to responsibly leave Iraq to its people and forge a hard- earned peace in Afghanistan.

With old friends and former foes, we'll work tirelessly to lessen the nuclear threat and roll back the specter of a warming planet.

We will not apologize for our way of life nor will we waver in its defense.

And for those who seek to advance their aims by inducing terror and slaughtering innocents, we say to you now that, "Our spirit is stronger and cannot be broken. You cannot outlast us, and we will defeat you."

(APPLAUSE)

For we know that our patchwork heritage is a strength, not a weakness.

We are a nation of Christians and Muslims, Jews and Hindus, and nonbelievers. We are shaped by every language and culture, drawn from every end of this Earth.

And because we have tasted the bitter swill of civil war and segregation and emerged from that dark chapter stronger and more united, we cannot help but believe that the old hatreds shall someday pass; that the lines of tribe shall soon dissolve; that as the world grows smaller, our common humanity shall reveal itself; and that America must play its role in ushering in a new era of peace.

To the Muslim world, we seek a new way forward, based on mutual interest and mutual respect.

To those leaders around the globe who seek to sow conflict or blame their society's ills on the West, know that your people will judge you on what you can build, not what you destroy.

To those...

(APPLAUSE)

To those who cling to power through corruption and deceit and the silencing of dissent, know that you are on the wrong side of history, but that we will extend a hand if you are willing to unclench your fist.

(APPLAUSE)

To the people of poor nations, we pledge to work alongside you to make your farms flourish and let clean waters flow; to nourish starved bodies and feed hungry minds.

And to those nations like ours that enjoy relative plenty, we say we can no longer afford indifference to the suffering outside our borders, nor can we consume the world's resources without regard to effect, for the world has changed, and we must change with it.

As we consider the road that unfolds before us, we remember with humble gratitude those brave Americans who, at this very hour, patrol far-off deserts and distant mountains. They have something to tell us, just as the fallen heroes who lie in Arlington whisper through the ages.

We honor them not only because they are guardians of our liberty, but because they embody the spirit of service: a willingness to find meaning in something greater than them.

And yet, at this moment, a moment that will define a generation, it is precisely this spirit that must inhabit us all.

For as much as government can do and must do, it is ultimately the faith and determination of the American people upon which this nation relies.

It is the kindness to take in a stranger when the levees break; the selflessness of workers who would rather cut their hours than see a friend lose their job which sees us through our darkest hours.

It is the firefighter's courage to storm a stairway filled with smoke, but also a parent's willingness to nurture a child, that finally decides our fate.

Our challenges may be new, the instruments with which we meet them may be new, but those values upon which our success depends, honesty and hard work, courage

and fair play, tolerance and curiosity, loyalty and patriotism --
these things are old.

These things are true. They have been the quiet force
of progress throughout our history.

What is demanded then is a return to these truths.
What is required of us now is a new era of responsibility -- a
recognition, on the part of every American, that we have
duties to ourselves, our nation and the world, duties that we
do not grudgingly accept but rather seize gladly, firm in the
knowledge that there is nothing so satisfying to the spirit, so
defining of our character than giving our all to a difficult task.

This is the price and the promise of citizenship.

This is the source of our confidence: the knowledge
that God calls on us to shape an uncertain destiny.

This is the meaning of our liberty and our creed, why
men and women and children of every race and every faith
can join in celebration across this magnificent mall. And why a
man whose father less than 60 years ago might not have been

served at a local restaurant can now stand before you to take a most sacred oath.

(APPLAUSE)

So let us mark this day in remembrance of who we are and how far we have traveled.

In the year of America's birth, in the coldest of months, a small band of patriots huddled by dying campfires on the shores of an icy river.

The capital was abandoned. The enemy was advancing. The snow was stained with blood.

At a moment when the outcome of our revolution was most in doubt, the father of our nation ordered these words be read to the people:

"Let it be told to the future world that in the depth of winter, when nothing but hope and virtue could survive, that the city and the country, alarmed at one common danger, came forth to meet it."

America, in the face of our common dangers, in this winter of our hardship, let us remember these timeless words;

with hope and virtue, let us brave once more the icy currents, and endure what storms may come; let it be said by our children's children that when we were tested we refused to let this journey end, that we did not turn back nor did we falter; and with eyes fixed on the horizon and God's grace upon us, we carried forth that great gift of freedom and delivered it safely to future generations.

Thank you. God bless you.

(APPLAUSE)

And God bless the United States of America.

Remarks of President Barack Obama

As Prepared for Delivery Address to Joint Session of Congress

Tuesday, February 24th, 2009

Madame Speaker, Mr. Vice President, Members of Congress, and the First Lady of the United States:

I've come here tonight not only to address the distinguished men and women in this great chamber, but to speak frankly and directly to the men and women who sent us here.

I know that for many Americans watching right now, the state of our economy is a concern that rises above all others. And rightly so, if you haven't been personally affected by this recession, you probably know someone who has – a friend; a neighbor; a member of your family. You don't need to hear another list of statistics to know that our economy is in crisis, because you live it every day. It's the worry you wake up with and the source of sleepless nights. It's the job you thought you'd retire from but now have lost; the business you built your dreams upon that are now hanging by a thread; the college acceptance letter your child had to put back in the envelope. The impact of this recession is real, and it is everywhere.

But while our economy may be weakened and our confidence shaken; though we are living through difficult and uncertain times, tonight I want every American to know this:

We will rebuild, we will recover, and the United States of America will emerge stronger than before.

The weight of this crisis will not determine the destiny of this nation. The answers to our problems don't lie beyond our reach. They exist in our laboratories and universities; in our fields and our factories; in the imaginations of our entrepreneurs and the pride of the hardest-working people on Earth. Those qualities that have made America the greatest force of progress and prosperity in human history we still possess in ample measure. What is required now is for this country to pull together, confront boldly the challenges we face, and take responsibility for our future once more.

Now, if we're honest with ourselves, we'll admit that for too long, we have not always met these responsibilities – as a government or as a people. I say this not to lay blame or look backwards, but because it is only by understanding how we arrived at this moment that we'll be able to lift ourselves out of this predicament.

The fact is, our economy did not fall into decline overnight. Nor did all of our problems begin when the housing market collapsed or the stock market sank. We have known for decades that our survival depends on finding new sources of energy. Yet we import more oil today than ever before. The cost of health care eats up more and more of our savings each year, yet we keep delaying reform. Our children will compete for jobs in a global economy that too many of our schools do not prepare them for. And though all these challenges went unsolved, we still managed to spend more money and pile up more debt, both as individuals and through our government, than ever before.

In other words, we have lived through an era where too often, short-term gains were prized over long-term prosperity; where we failed to look beyond the next payment, the next quarter, or the next election. A surplus became an excuse to transfer wealth to the wealthy instead of an opportunity to invest in our future. Regulations were gutted for the sake of a quick profit at the expense of a healthy market. People bought homes they knew they couldn't afford from banks and lenders who pushed those bad loans anyway. And all the while, critical debates and difficult decisions were put off for some other time on some other day.

Well that day of reckoning has arrived, and the time to take charge of our future is here.

Now is the time to act boldly and wisely – to not only revive this economy, but to build a new foundation for lasting prosperity. Now is the time to jumpstart job creation, re-start lending, and invest in areas like energy, health care, and education that will grow our economy, even as we make hard choices to bring our deficit down. That is what my economic agenda is designed to do, and that's what I'd like to talk to you about tonight.

It's an agenda that begins with jobs.

As soon as I took office, I asked this Congress to send me a recovery plan by President's Day that would put people back to work and put money in their pockets. Not because I believe in bigger government – I don't. Not because I'm not mindful of the massive debt we've inherited – I am. I called for action because the failure to do so would have cost more jobs and caused more hardships. In fact, a failure to act would have worsened our long-term deficit by assuring weak economic growth for years. That's why I pushed for quick action. And tonight, I am grateful that this Congress delivered, and pleased to say that the American Recovery and Reinvestment Act is now law.

Over the next two years, this plan will save or create 3.5 million jobs. More than 90% of these jobs will be in the private sector – jobs rebuilding our roads and bridges; constructing wind turbines and solar panels; laying broadband and expanding mass transit.

Because of this plan, there are teachers who can now keep their jobs and educate our kids. Health care professionals can continue caring for our sick. There are 57 police officers who are still on the streets of Minneapolis tonight because this plan prevented the layoffs their department was about to make.

Because of this plan, 95% of the working households in America will receive a tax cut – a tax cut that you will see in your paychecks beginning on April 1st.

Because of this plan, families who are struggling to pay tuition costs will receive a $2,500 tax credit for all four years of college. And Americans who have lost their jobs in this recession will be able to receive extended unemployment benefits and continued health care coverage to help them weather this storm.

I know there are some in this chamber and watching at home who are skeptical of whether this plan will work. I understand that skepticism. Here in Washington, we've all seen how quickly good intentions can turn into broken promises and wasteful spending. And with a plan of this scale comes enormous responsibility to get it right.

That is why I have asked Vice President Biden to lead a tough, unprecedented oversight effort – because nobody messes with Joe. I have told each member of my Cabinet as well as mayors and governors across the country that they will be held accountable by me and the American people for every dollar they spend. I have appointed a proven and aggressive Inspector General to ferret out any and all cases of waste and fraud. And we have created a new website called recovery.gov so that every American can find out how and where their money is being spent.

So the recovery plan we passed is the first step in getting our economy back on track. But it is just the first step. Because even if we manage this plan flawlessly, there will be no real recovery unless we clean up the credit crisis that has severely weakened our financial system.

I want to speak plainly and candidly about this issue tonight, because every American should know that it directly affects you and your family's well-being. You should also know that the money you've deposited in banks across the country is safe; your insurance is secure; and you can rely on the continued operation of our financial system. That is not the source of concern.

The concern is that if we do not re-start lending in this country, our recovery will be choked off before it even begins.

You see, the flow of credit is the lifeblood of our economy. The ability to get a loan is how you finance the purchase of everything from a home to a car to a college education; how stores stock their shelves, farms buy equipment, and businesses make payroll.

But credit has stopped flowing the way it should. Too many bad loans from the housing crisis have made their way onto the books of too many banks. With so much debt and so little confidence, these banks are now fearful of lending out any more money to households, to businesses, or to each other. When there is no lending, families can't afford to buy homes or cars. So businesses are forced to make layoffs. Our economy suffers even more, and credit dries up even further.

That is why this administration is moving swiftly and aggressively to break this destructive cycle, restore confidence, and re-start lending.

We will do so in several ways. First, we are creating a new lending fund that represents the largest effort ever to help provide auto loans, college loans, and small business loans to the consumers and entrepreneurs who keep this economy running.

Second, we have launched a housing plan that will help responsible families facing the threat of foreclosure lower their monthly payments and re-finance their mortgages. It's a plan that won't help speculators or that neighbor down the street who bought a house he could never hope to afford, but it will help millions of Americans who are struggling with declining home values – Americans who will now be able to take advantage of the lower interest rates that this plan has already helped bring about. In fact, the average family who re-finances today can save nearly $2000 per year on their mortgage.

Third, we will act with the full force of the federal government to ensure that the major banks that Americans depend on have enough confidence and enough money to lend even in more difficult times. And when we learn that a major bank has serious problems, we will hold accountable those responsible, force the necessary adjustments, provide the support to clean up their balance sheets, and assure the continuity of a strong, viable institution that can serve our people and our economy.

I understand that on any given day, Wall Street may be more comforted by an approach that gives banks bailouts with no strings attached, and that holds nobody accountable for their reckless decisions. But such an approach won't solve the problem. And our goal is to quicken the day when we re-start lending to the American people and American business and end this crisis once and for all.

I intend to hold these banks fully accountable for the assistance they receive, and this time, they will have to clearly demonstrate how taxpayer dollars result in more lending for the American taxpayer. This time, CEOs won't be able to use taxpayer money to pad their paychecks or buy fancy drapes or disappear on a private jet. Those days are over.

Still, this plan will require significant resources from the federal government – and yes, probably more than we've already set aside. But while the cost of action will be great, I can assure you that the cost of inaction will be far greater, for it could result in an economy that sputters along for not months or years, but perhaps a decade. That would be worse for our deficit, worse for business, worse for you and worse for the next generation. And I refuse to let that happen.

I understand that when the last administration asked this Congress to provide assistance for struggling banks, Democrats and Republicans alike were infuriated by the mismanagement and results that followed. So were the American taxpayers. So was I.

So I know how unpopular it is to be seen as helping banks right now, especially when everyone is suffering in part from their bad decisions. I promise you – I get it.

But I also know that in a time of crisis, we cannot afford to govern out of anger, or yield to the politics of the moment. My job – our job – is to solve the problem. Our job is to govern with a sense of responsibility. I will not spend a single penny for the purpose of rewarding a single Wall Street executive, but I will do whatever it takes to help the small business that can't pay its workers or the family that has saved and still can't get a mortgage.

That's what this is about. It's not about helping banks – it's about helping people. Because when credit is available again, that young family can finally buy a new home. And then some company will hire workers to build it. And then those workers will have money to spend, and if they can get a loan too, maybe they'll finally buy that car, or open their own business. Investors will return to the market, and American families will see their retirement secured once more. Slowly, but surely, confidence will return, and our economy will recover.

So I ask this Congress to join me in doing whatever proves necessary. Because we cannot consign our nation to an open-ended recession. And to ensure that a crisis of this magnitude never happens again, I ask Congress to move quickly on legislation that will finally reform our outdated regulatory system. It is time to put in place tough, new common-sense rules of the road so that our financial market rewards drive and innovation, and punishes short-cuts and abuse.

The recovery plan and the financial stability plan are the immediate steps we're taking to revive our economy in the short-term. But the only way to fully restore America's economic strength is to make the long-term investments that will lead to new jobs, new industries, and a renewed ability to compete with the rest of the world. The only way this century will be another American century is if we confront at last the price of our dependence on oil and the high cost of health care; the schools that aren't preparing our children and the mountain of debt they stand to inherit. That is our responsibility.

In the next few days, I will submit a budget to Congress. So often, we have come to view these documents as simply numbers on a page or laundry lists of programs. I see this document differently. I see it as a vision for America – as a blueprint for our future.

My budget does not attempt to solve every problem or address every issue. It reflects the stark reality of what we've inherited – a trillion dollar deficit, a financial crisis, and a costly recession.

Given these realities, everyone in this chamber – Democrats and Republicans – will have to sacrifice some worthy priorities for which there are no dollars. And that includes me.

But that does not mean we can afford to ignore our long-term challenges. I reject the view that says our problems will simply take care of themselves; that says government has no role in laying the foundation for our common prosperity.

For history tells a different story. History reminds us that at every moment of economic upheaval and transformation, this nation has responded with bold action and big ideas. In the midst of civil war, we laid railroad tracks from one coast to another that spurred commerce and industry. From the turmoil of the Industrial Revolution came a system of public high schools that prepared our citizens for a new age. In the wake of war and depression, the GI Bill sent a generation to college and created the largest middle-class in history. And a twilight struggle for freedom led to a nation of highways, an American on the moon, and an explosion of technology that still shapes our world.

In each case, government didn't supplant private enterprise; it catalyzed private enterprise. It created the conditions for thousands of entrepreneurs and new businesses to adapt and to thrive.

We are a nation that has seen promise amid peril, and claimed opportunity from ordeal. Now we must be that nation again. That is why, even as it cuts back on the programs we don't need, the budget I submit will invest in the three areas that are absolutely critical to our economic future: energy, health care, and education.

It begins with energy.

We know the country that harnesses the power of clean, renewable energy will lead the 21st century. And yet, it is China that has launched the largest effort in history to make their economy energy efficient. We invented solar technology, but we've fallen behind countries like Germany and Japan in producing it. New plug-in hybrids roll off our assembly lines, but they will run on batteries made in Korea.

Well I do not accept a future where the jobs and industries of tomorrow take root beyond our borders – and I know you don't either. It is time for America to lead again.

Thanks to our recovery plan, we will double this nation's supply of renewable energy in the next three years. We have also made the largest investment in basic research funding in American history – an investment that will spur not only new discoveries in energy, but breakthroughs in medicine, science, and technology.

We will soon lay down thousands of miles of power lines that can carry new energy to cities and towns across this country. And we will put Americans to work making our homes and buildings more efficient so that we can save billions of dollars on our energy bills.

But to truly transform our economy, protect our security, and save our planet from the ravages of climate change, we need to ultimately make clean, renewable energy the profitable kind of energy. So I ask this Congress to send me legislation that places a market-based cap on carbon pollution and drives the production of more renewable energy in America. And to support that innovation, we will invest fifteen billion dollars a year to develop technologies like wind power and solar power; advanced biofuels, clean coal, and more fuel-efficient cars and trucks built right here in America.

As for our auto industry, everyone recognizes that years of bad decision-making and a global recession have pushed our automakers to the brink. We should not, and will not, protect them from their own bad practices. But we are committed to the goal of a re-tooled, re-imagined auto industry that can compete and win. Millions of jobs depend on it. Scores of communities depend on it. And I believe the nation that invented the automobile cannot walk away from it.

None of this will come without cost, nor will it be easy. But this is America. We don't do what's easy. We do what is necessary to move this country forward.

For that same reason, we must also address the crushing cost of health care.

This is a cost that now causes a bankruptcy in America every thirty seconds. By the end of the year, it could cause 1.5 million Americans to lose their homes. In the last eight years, premiums have grown four times faster than wages. And in each of these years, one million more Americans have lost their health insurance. It is one of the major reasons why small businesses close their doors and corporations ship jobs overseas. And it's one of the largest and fastest-growing parts of our budget.

Given these facts, we can no longer afford to put health care reform on hold.

Already, we have done more to advance the cause of health care reform in the last thirty days than we have in the last decade. When it was days old, this Congress passed a law to provide and protect health insurance for eleven million American children whose parents work full-time. Our recovery plan will invest in electronic health records and new technology that will reduce errors, bring down costs, ensure privacy, and save lives. It will launch a new effort to conquer a disease that has touched the life of nearly every American by seeking a cure for cancer in our time. And it makes the largest investment ever in preventive care, because that is one of the best ways to keep our people healthy and our costs under control.

This budget builds on these reforms. It includes an historic commitment to comprehensive health care reform – a down-payment on the principle that we must have quality, affordable health care for every American. It's a commitment that's paid for in part by efficiencies in our system that are long overdue. And it's a step we must take if we hope to bring down our deficit in the years to come.

Now, there will be many different opinions and ideas about how to achieve reform, and that is why I'm bringing together businesses and workers, doctors and health care providers, Democrats and Republicans to begin work on this issue next week.

I suffer no illusions that this will be an easy process. It will be hard. But I also know that nearly a century after Teddy Roosevelt first called for reform, the cost of our health care has weighed down our economy and the conscience of our nation long enough. So let there be no doubt: health care reform cannot wait, it must not wait, and it will not wait another year.

The third challenge we must address is the urgent need to expand the promise of education in America.

In a global economy where the most valuable skill you can sell is your knowledge, a good education is no longer just a pathway to opportunity – it is a pre-requisite.

Right now, three-quarters of the fastest-growing occupations require more than a high school diploma. And yet, just over half of our citizens have that level of education. We have one of the highest high school dropout rates of any industrialized nation. And half of the students who begin college never finish.

This is a prescription for economic decline, because we know the countries that out-teach us today will out-compete us tomorrow. That is why it will be the goal of this administration to ensure that every child has access to a complete and competitive education – from the day they are born to the day they begin a career.

Already, we have made an historic investment in education through the economic recovery plan. We have dramatically expanded early childhood education and will continue to improve its quality, because we know that the most formative learning comes in those first years of life. We have made college affordable for nearly seven million more students. And we have provided the resources necessary to prevent painful cuts and teacher layoffs that would set back our children's progress.

But we know that our schools don't just need more resources. They need more reform. That is why this budget creates new incentives for teacher performance; pathways for advancement, and rewards for success. We'll invest in innovative programs that are already helping schools meet high standards and close achievement gaps. And we will expand our commitment to charter schools.

It is our responsibility as lawmakers and educators to make this system work. But it is the responsibility of every citizen to participate in it. And so tonight, I ask every American to commit to at least one year or more of higher education or career training. This can be community college or a four-year school; vocational training or an apprenticeship. But whatever the training may be, every American will need to get more than a high school diploma. And dropping out of high school is no longer an option. It's not just quitting on yourself, it's quitting on your country – and this country needs and values the talents of every American. That is why we will provide the support necessary for you to complete college and meet a new goal: by 2020, America will once again have the highest proportion of college graduates in the world.

I know that the price of tuition is higher than ever, which is why if you are willing to volunteer in your neighborhood or give back to your community or serve your country, we will make sure that you can afford a higher education. And to encourage a renewed spirit of national service for this and future generations, I ask this Congress to send me the bipartisan legislation that bears the name of Senator Orrin Hatch as well as an American who has never stopped asking what he can do for his country – Senator Edward Kennedy.

These education policies will open the doors of opportunity for our children. But it is up to us to ensure they walk through them. In the end, there is no program or policy that can substitute for a mother or father who will attend those parent/teacher conferences, or help with homework after dinner, or turn off the TV, put away the video games, and read to their child. I speak to you not just as a President, but as a father when I say that responsibility for our children's education must begin at home.

There is, of course, another responsibility we have to our children. And that is the responsibility to ensure that we do not pass on to them a debt they cannot pay. With the deficit we inherited, the cost of the crisis we face, and the long-term challenges we must meet, it has never been more important to ensure that as our economy recovers, we do what it takes to bring this deficit down.

I'm proud that we passed the recovery plan free of earmarks, and I want to pass a budget next year that ensures that each dollar we spend reflects only our most important national priorities.

Yesterday, I held a fiscal summit where I pledged to cut the deficit in half by the end of my first term in office. My administration has also begun to go line by line through the federal budget in order to eliminate wasteful and ineffective programs. As you can imagine, this is a process that will take some time. But we're starting with the biggest lines. We have already identified two trillion dollars in savings over the next decade.

In this budget, we will end education programs that don't work and end direct payments to large agribusinesses that don't need them. We'll eliminate the no-bid contracts that have wasted billions in Iraq, and reform our defense budget so that we're not paying for Cold War-era weapons systems we don't use. We will root out the waste, fraud, and abuse in our Medicare program that doesn't make our seniors any healthier, and we will restore a sense of fairness and balance to our tax code by finally ending the tax breaks for corporations that ship our jobs overseas.

In order to save our children from a future of debt, we will also end the tax breaks for the wealthiest 2% of Americans. But let me perfectly clear, because I know you'll hear the same old claims that rolling back these tax breaks means a massive tax increase on the American people: if your family earns less than $250,000 a year, you will not see your taxes increased a single dime. I repeat: not one single dime. In fact, the recovery plan provides a tax cut – that's right, a tax cut – for 95% of working families. And these checks are on the way.

To preserve our long-term fiscal health, we must also address the growing costs in Medicare and Social Security. Comprehensive health care reform is the best way to strengthen Medicare for years to come. And we must also begin a conversation on how to do the same for Social

Security, while creating tax-free universal savings accounts for all Americans.

Finally, because we're also suffering from a deficit of trust, I am committed to restoring a sense of honesty and accountability to our budget. That is why this budget looks ahead ten years and accounts for spending that was left out under the old rules – and for the first time, that includes the full cost of fighting in Iraq and Afghanistan. For seven years, we have been a nation at war. No longer will we hide its price.

We are now carefully reviewing our policies in both wars, and I will soon announce a way forward in Iraq that leaves Iraq to its people and responsibly ends this war.

And with our friends and allies, we will forge a new and comprehensive strategy for Afghanistan and Pakistan to defeat al Qaeda and combat extremism. Because I will not allow terrorists to plot against the American people from safe havens half a world away.

As we meet here tonight, our men and women in uniform stand watch abroad and more are readying to deploy.

To each and every one of them, and to the families who bear the quiet burden of their absence, Americans are united in sending one message: we honor your service, we are inspired by your sacrifice, and you have our unyielding support. To relieve the strain on our forces, my budget increases the number of our soldiers and Marines. And to keep our sacred trust with those who serve, we will raise their pay, and give our veterans the expanded health care and benefits that they have earned.

To overcome extremism, we must also be vigilant in upholding the values our troops defend – because there is no force in the world more powerful than the example of America. That is why I have ordered the closing of the detention center at Guantanamo Bay, and will seek swift and certain justice for captured terrorists – because living our values doesn't make us weaker, it makes us safer and it makes us stronger. And that is why I can stand here tonight and say without exception or equivocation that the United States of America does not torture.

In words and deeds, we are showing the world that a new era of engagement has begun. For we know that America cannot meet the threats of this century alone, but the world cannot meet them without America. We cannot shun the negotiating table, nor ignore the foes or forces that could do us harm. We are instead called to move forward with the sense of confidence and candor that serious times demand.

To seek progress toward a secure and lasting peace between Israel and her neighbors, we have appointed an envoy to sustain our effort. To meet the challenges of the 21st century – from terrorism to nuclear proliferation; from pandemic disease to cyber threats to crushing poverty – we will strengthen old alliances, forge new ones, and use all elements of our national power.

And to respond to an economic crisis that is global in scope, we are working with the nations of the G-20 to restore confidence in our financial system, avoid the possibility of escalating protectionism, and spur demand for American goods in markets across the globe. For the world depends on us to have a strong economy, just as our economy depends on the strength of the world's.

As we stand at this crossroads of history, the eyes of all people in all nations are once again upon us – watching to see what we do with this moment; waiting for us to lead.

Those of us gathered here tonight have been called to govern in extraordinary times. It is a tremendous burden, but also a great privilege – one that has been entrusted to few generations of Americans. For in our hands lies the ability to shape our world for good or for ill.

I know that it is easy to lose sight of this truth – to become cynical and doubtful; consumed with the petty and the trivial.

But in my life, I have also learned that hope is found in unlikely places; that inspiration often comes not from those with the most power or celebrity, but from the dreams and aspirations of Americans who are anything but ordinary.

I think about Leonard Abbess, the bank president from Miami who reportedly cashed out of his company, took a $60 million bonus, and gave it out to all 399 people who worked for him, plus another 72 who used to work for him. He didn't tell anyone, but when the local newspaper found out, he simply said, "I knew some of these people since I was 7 years old. I didn't feel right getting the money myself."

I think about Greensburg, Kansas, a town that was completely destroyed by a tornado, but is being rebuilt by its residents as a global example of how clean energy can power an entire community – how it can bring jobs and businesses to a place where piles of bricks and rubble once lay. "The tragedy was terrible," said one of the men who helped them rebuild. "But the folks here know that it also provided an incredible opportunity."

And I think about Ty'Sheoma Bethea, the young girl from that school I visited in Dillon, South Carolina – a place where the ceilings leak, the paint peels off the walls, and they have to stop teaching six times a day because the train barrels by their classroom. She has been told that her school is hopeless, but the other day after class she went to the public library and typed up a letter to the people sitting in this room. She even asked her principal for the money to buy a stamp. The letter asks us for help, and says, "We are just students trying to become lawyers, doctors, congressmen like yourself and one day president, so we can make a change to not just the state of South Carolina but also the world. We are not quitters."

We are not quitters.

These words and these stories tell us something about the spirit of the people who sent us here. They tell us that even in the most trying times, amid the most difficult circumstances, there is a generosity, a resilience, a decency, and a determination that perseveres; a willingness to take responsibility for our future and for posterity.

Their resolve must be our inspiration. Their concerns must be our cause. And we must show them and all our people that we are equal to the task before us.

I know that we haven't agreed on every issue thus far, and there are surely times in the future when we will part ways. But I also know that every American who is sitting here tonight loves this country and wants it to succeed. That must be the starting point for every debate we have in the coming months, and where we return after those debates are done. That is the foundation on which the American people expect us to build common ground.

And if we do – if we come together and lift this nation from the depths of this crisis; if we put our people back to work and restart the engine of our prosperity; if we confront without fear the challenges of our time and summon that enduring spirit of an America that does not quit, then someday years from now our children can tell their children that this was the time when we performed, in the words that are carved into this very chamber, "something worthy to be remembered." Thank you, God Bless you, and may God Bless the United States of America.

Remarks by the President in State of the Union Address

United States Capitol

Washington, D.C.

9:10 P.M. EST

THE PRESIDENT: Mr. Speaker, Mr. Vice President, members of Congress, distinguished guests, and fellow Americans:

Last month, I went to Andrews Air Force Base and welcomed home some of our last troops to serve in Iraq. Together, we offered a final, proud salute to the colors under which more than a million of our fellow citizens fought -- and several thousand gave their lives.

We gather tonight knowing that this generation of heroes has made the United States safer and more respected around the world.

(Applause.)

For the first time in nine years, there are no Americans fighting in Iraq.

(Applause.)

For the first time in two decades, Osama bin Laden is not a threat to this country.

(Applause.)

Most of al Qaeda's top lieutenants have been defeated. The Taliban's momentum has been broken, and some troops in Afghanistan have begun to come home.

These achievements are a testament to the courage, selflessness and teamwork of America's Armed Forces. At a time when too many of our institutions have let us down, they exceed all expectations. They're not consumed with personal ambition. They don't obsess over their differences. They focus on the mission at hand. They work together.

Imagine what we could accomplish if we followed their example.

(Applause.)

Think about the America within our reach: A country that leads the world in educating its people. An America that attracts a new generation of high-tech manufacturing and high-paying jobs. A future where we're in control of our own energy, and our security and prosperity aren't so tied to unstable parts of the world. An economy built to last, where hard work pays off, and responsibility is rewarded.

We can do this. I know we can, because we've done it before. At the end of World War II, when another generation of heroes returned home from combat, they built the strongest economy and middle class the world has ever known.

(Applause.)

My grandfather, a veteran of Patton's Army, got the chance to go to college on the GI Bill. My grandmother, who worked on a bomber assembly line, was part of a workforce that turned out the best products on Earth.

The two of them shared the optimism of a nation that had triumphed over a depression and fascism. They understood they were part of something larger; that they were contributing to a story of success that every American had a chance to share -- the basic American promise that if you worked hard, you could do well enough to raise a family, own a home, send your kids to college, and put a little away for retirement.

The defining issue of our time is how to keep that promise alive. No challenge is more urgent. No debate is more important. We can either settle for a country where a shrinking number of people do really well while a growing number of Americans barely get by, or we can restore an economy where everyone gets a fair shot, and everyone does their fair share, and everyone plays by the same set of rules. (Applause.) What's at stake aren't Democratic values or

Republican values, but American values. And we have to reclaim them.

Let's remember how we got here. Long before the recession, jobs and manufacturing began leaving our shores. Technology made businesses more efficient, but also made some jobs obsolete. Folks at the top saw their incomes rise like never before, but most hardworking Americans struggled with costs that were growing, paychecks that weren't, and personal debt that kept piling up.

In 2008, the house of cards collapsed. We learned that mortgages had been sold to people who couldn't afford or understand them. Banks had made huge bets and bonuses with other people's money. Regulators had looked the other way, or didn't have the authority to stop the bad behavior.

It was wrong. It was irresponsible. And it plunged our economy into a crisis that put millions out of work, saddled us with more debt, and left innocent, hardworking Americans holding the bag. In the six months before I took office, we lost nearly 4 million jobs. And we lost another 4 million before our policies were in full effect.

Those are the facts. But so are these: In the last 22 months, businesses have created more than 3 million jobs. (Applause.)

Last year, they created the most jobs since 2005. American manufacturers are hiring again, creating jobs for the first time since the late 1990s. Together, we've agreed to cut the deficit by more than $2 trillion. And we've put in place new rules to hold Wall Street accountable, so a crisis like this never happens again. (Applause.)

The state of our Union is getting stronger. And we've come too far to turn back now. As long as I'm President, I will work with anyone in this chamber to build on this momentum. But I intend to fight obstruction with action, and I will oppose any effort to return to the very same policies that brought on this economic crisis in the first place. (Applause.)

No, we will not go back to an economy weakened by outsourcing, bad debt, and phony financial profits. Tonight, I want to speak about how we move forward, and lay out a blueprint for an economy that's built to last — an economy built on American manufacturing, American energy, skills for American workers, and a renewal of American values.

Now, this blueprint begins with American manufacturing.

On the day I took office, our auto industry was on the verge of collapse. Some even said we should let it die. With a million jobs at stake, I refused to let that happen. In exchange for help, we demanded responsibility. We got workers and automakers to settle their differences. We got the industry to retool and restructure. Today, General Motors is back on top as the world's number-one automaker. (Applause.) Chrysler has grown faster in the U.S. than any major car company. Ford is investing billions in U.S. plants and factories. And together, the entire industry added nearly 160,000 jobs.

We bet on American workers. We bet on American ingenuity. And tonight, the American auto industry is back. (Applause.)

What's happening in Detroit can happen in other industries. It can happen in Cleveland and Pittsburgh and Raleigh. We can't bring every job back that's left our shore. But right now, it's getting more expensive to do business in places like China. Meanwhile, America is more productive. A few weeks ago, the CEO of Master Lock told me that it now makes business sense for him to bring jobs back home. (Applause.)

Today, for the first time in 15 years, Master Lock's unionized plant in Milwaukee is running at full capacity. (Applause.)

So we have a huge opportunity, at this moment, to bring manufacturing back. But we have to seize it. Tonight, my message to business leaders is simple: Ask yourselves what you can do to bring jobs back to your country, and your country will do everything we can to help you succeed. (Applause.)

We should start with our tax code. Right now, companies get tax breaks for moving jobs and profits overseas. Meanwhile, companies that choose to stay in America get hit with one of the highest tax rates in the world. It makes no sense, and everyone knows it. So let's change it.

First, if you're a business that wants to outsource jobs, you shouldn't get a tax deduction for doing it.

(Applause.)

That money should be used to cover moving expenses for companies like Master Lock that decide to bring jobs home. (Applause.)

Second, no American company should be able to avoid paying its fair share of taxes by moving jobs and profits overseas.

(Applause.)

From now on, every multinational company should have to pay a basic minimum tax. And every penny should go towards lowering taxes for companies that choose to stay here and hire here in America.

(Applause.)

Third, if you're an American manufacturer, you should get a bigger tax cut. If you're a high-tech manufacturer, we should double the tax deduction you get for making your products here. And if you want to relocate in a community that was hit hard when a factory left town, you should get help financing a new plant, equipment, or training for new workers. (Applause.)

So my message is simple. It is time to stop rewarding businesses that ship jobs overseas, and start rewarding companies that create jobs right here in America. Send me these tax reforms, and I will sign them right away.

(Applause.)

We're also making it easier for American businesses to sell products all over the world. Two years ago, I set a goal of doubling U.S. exports over five years. With the bipartisan trade agreements we signed into law, we're on track to meet that goal ahead of schedule. (Applause.) And soon, there will be millions of new customers for American goods in Panama, Colombia, and South Korea. Soon, there will be new cars on the streets of Seoul imported from Detroit, and Toledo, and Chicago.

(Applause.)

I will go anywhere in the world to open new markets for American products. And I will not stand by when our competitors don't play by the rules. We've brought trade cases against China at nearly twice the rate as the last administration –- and it's made a difference.

(Applause.)

Over a thousand Americans are working today because we stopped a surge in Chinese tires. But we need to do more. It's not right when another country lets our movies, music, and software be pirated. It's not fair when foreign manufacturers have a leg up on ours only because they're heavily subsidized.

Tonight, I'm announcing the creation of a Trade Enforcement Unit that will be charged with investigating unfair trading practices in countries like China.

(Applause.)

There will be more inspections to prevent counterfeit or unsafe goods from crossing our borders. And this Congress should make sure that no foreign company has an advantage over American manufacturing when it comes to accessing financing or new markets like Russia. Our workers are the most productive on Earth, and if the playing field is level, I promise you — America will always win.

(Applause.)

I also hear from many business leaders who want to hire in the United States but can't find workers with the right skills. Growing industries in science and technology have twice as many openings as we have workers who can do the job. Think about that — openings at a time when millions of Americans are looking for work. It's inexcusable. And we know how to fix it.

Jackie Bray is a single mom from North Carolina who was laid off from her job as a mechanic. Then Siemens opened a gas turbine factory in Charlotte, and formed a partnership with Central Piedmont Community College. The company helped the college design courses in laser and robotics training. It paid Jackie's tuition, and then hired her to help operate their plant.

I want every American looking for work to have the same opportunity as Jackie did. Join me in a national commitment to train 2 million Americans with skills that will lead directly to a job.

(Applause.)

My administration has already lined up more companies that want to help. Model partnerships between businesses like Siemens and community colleges in places like Charlotte, and Orlando, and Louisville are up and running, now you need to give more community colleges the resources they need to become community career centers — places that teach people skills that businesses are looking for right now, from data management to high-tech manufacturing.

And I want to cut through the maze of confusing training programs, so that from now on, people like Jackie have one program, one website, and one place to go for all the information and help that they need. It is time to turn our unemployment system into a reemployment system that puts people to work. (Applause.)

These reforms will help people get jobs that are open today. But to prepare for the jobs of tomorrow, our commitment to skills and education has to start earlier.

For less than 1 percent of what our nation spends on education each year, we've convinced nearly every state in the country to raise their standards for teaching and learning - - the first time that's happened in a generation.

But challenges remain. And we know how to solve them.

At a time when other countries are doubling down on education, tight budgets have forced states to lay off thousands of teachers. We know a good teacher can increase the lifetime income of a classroom by over $250,000. A great teacher can offer an escape from poverty to the child who dreams beyond his circumstance. Every person in this chamber can point to a teacher who changed the trajectory of their lives. Most teachers work tirelessly, with modest pay, sometimes digging into their own pocket for school supplies -- just to make a difference.

Teachers matter. So instead of bashing them, or defending the status quo, let's offer schools a deal. Give them the resources to keep good teachers on the job, and reward the best ones.

(Applause.)

And in return, grant schools flexibility: to teach with creativity and passion; to stop teaching to the test; and to replace teachers who just aren't helping kids learn. That's a bargain worth making.

(Applause.)

We also know that when students don't walk away from their education, more of them walk the stage to get their diploma. When students are not allowed to drop out, they do better. So tonight, I am proposing that every state -- every state -- requires that all students stay in high school until they graduate or turn 18.

(Applause.)

When kids do graduate, the most daunting challenge can be the cost of college. At a time when Americans owe more in tuition debt than credit card debt, this Congress needs to stop the interest rates on student loans from doubling in July. (Applause.)

Extend the tuition tax credit we started that saves millions of middle-class families thousands of dollars, and give more young people the chance to earn their way through college by doubling the number of work-study jobs in the next five years.

(Applause.)

Of course, it's not enough for us to increase student aid. We can't just keep subsidizing skyrocketing tuition; we'll run out of money. States also need to do their part, by making higher education a higher priority in their budgets. And colleges and universities have to do their part by working to keep costs down.

Recently, I spoke with a group of college presidents who've done just that. Some schools redesign courses to help students finish more quickly. Some use better technology. The point is, it's possible. So let me put colleges and universities on notice: If you can't stop tuition from going up, the funding you get from taxpayers will go down.

(Applause.)

Higher education can't be a luxury — it is an economic imperative that every family in America should be able to afford.

Let's also remember that hundreds of thousands of talented, hardworking students in this country face another challenge: the fact that they aren't yet American citizens.

Many were brought here as small children, are American through and through, yet they live every day with the threat of deportation. Others came more recently, to study business and science and engineering, but as soon as they get their degree, we send them home to invent new products and create new jobs somewhere else.

That doesn't make sense.

I believe as strongly as ever that we should take on illegal immigration. That's why my administration has put more boots on the border than ever before. That's why there are fewer illegal crossings than when I took office. The opponents of action are out of excuses. We should be working on comprehensive immigration reform right now.

(Applause.)

But if election-year politics keeps Congress from acting on a comprehensive plan, let's at least agree to stop expelling responsible young people who want to staff our labs, start new businesses, and defend this country. Send me a law that gives them the chance to earn their citizenship. I will sign it right away. (Applause.)

You see, an economy built to last is one where we encourage the talent and ingenuity of every person in this country. That means women should earn equal pay for equal work. (Applause.) It means we should support everyone who's willing to work, and every risk-taker and entrepreneur who aspires to become the next Steve Jobs.

After all, innovation is what America has always been about. Most new jobs are created in start-ups and small businesses. So let's pass an agenda that helps them succeed. Tear down regulations that prevent aspiring entrepreneurs from getting the financing to grow.

(Applause.) Expand tax relief to small businesses that are raising wages and creating good jobs. Both parties agree on these ideas. So put them in a bill, and get it on my desk this year.

(Applause.)

Innovation also demands basic research. Today, the discoveries taking place in our federally financed labs and universities could lead to new treatments that kill cancer cells but leave healthy ones untouched. New lightweight vests for cops and soldiers that can stop any bullet. Don't gut these investments in our budget. Don't let other countries win the race for the future. Support the same kind of research and innovation that led to the computer chip and the Internet; to new American jobs and new American industries.

And nowhere is the promise of innovation greater than in American-made energy. Over the last three years, we've opened millions of new acres for oil and gas exploration, and tonight, I'm directing my administration to open more than 75 percent of our potential offshore oil and gas resources. (Applause.) Right now -- right now -- American oil production is the highest that it's been in eight years. That's right -- eight years. Not only that -- last year, we relied less on foreign oil than in any of the past 16 years. (Applause.)

But with only 2 percent of the world's oil reserves, oil isn't enough. This country needs an all-out, all-of-the-above strategy that develops every available source of American energy.

(Applause.)

A strategy that's cleaner, cheaper, and full of new jobs.

We have a supply of natural gas that can last America nearly 100 years.

(Applause.)

And my administration will take every possible action to safely develop this energy. Experts believe this will support more than 600,000 jobs by the end of the decade. And I'm requiring all companies that drill for gas on public lands to disclose the chemicals they use. (Applause.) Because America will develop this resource without putting the health and safety of our citizens at risk.

The development of natural gas will create jobs and power trucks and factories that are cleaner and cheaper, proving that we don't have to choose between our environment and our economy.

(Applause.) And by the way, it was public research dollars, over the course of 30 years, that helped develop the technologies to extract all this natural gas out of shale rock –- reminding us that government support is critical in helping businesses get new energy ideas off the ground.

(Applause.)

Now, what's true for natural gas is just as true for clean energy. In three years, our partnership with the private sector has already positioned America to be the world's leading manufacturer of high-tech batteries. Because of federal investments, renewable energy use has nearly doubled, and thousands of Americans have jobs because of it.

When Bryan Ritterby was laid off from his job making furniture, he said he worried that at 55, no one would give him a second chance. But he found work at Energetx, a wind turbine manufacturer in Michigan. Before the recession, the factory only made luxury yachts.

Today, it's hiring workers like Bryan, who said, "I'm proud to be working in the industry of the future."

Our experience with shale gas, our experience with natural gas, shows us that the payoffs on these public investments don't always come right away. Some technologies don't pan out; some companies fail. But I will not walk away from the promise of clean energy. I will not walk away from workers like Bryan.

(Applause.)

I will not cede the wind or solar or battery industry to China or Germany because we refuse to make the same commitment here.

We've subsidized oil companies for a century. That's long enough.

(Applause.)

It's time to end the taxpayer giveaways to an industry that rarely has been more profitable, and double-down on a clean energy industry that never has been more promising. Pass clean energy tax credits. Create these jobs.

(Applause.)

We can also spur energy innovation with new incentives. The differences in this chamber may be too deep right now to pass a comprehensive plan to fight climate change. But there's no reason why Congress shouldn't at least set a clean energy standard that creates a market for innovation. So far, you haven't acted. Well, tonight, I will. I'm directing my administration to allow the development of clean energy on enough public land to power 3 million homes. And I'm proud to announce that the Department of Defense, working with us, the world's largest consumer of energy, will make one of the largest commitments to clean energy in history - with the Navy purchasing enough capacity to power a quarter of a million homes a year.

(Applause.)

Of course, the easiest way to save money is to waste less energy. So here's a proposal: Help manufacturers eliminate energy waste in their factories and give businesses incentives to upgrade their buildings. Their energy bills will be $100 billion lower over the next decade, and America will have less pollution, more manufacturing, more jobs for construction workers who need them. Send me a bill that creates these jobs.

(Applause.)

Building this new energy future should be just one part of a broader agenda to repair America's infrastructure. So much of America needs to be rebuilt. We've got crumbling roads and bridges; a power grid that wastes too much energy; an incomplete high-speed broadband network that prevents a small business owner in rural America from selling her products all over the world.

During the Great Depression, America built the Hoover Dam and the Golden Gate Bridge. After World War II, we connected our states with a system of highways. Democratic and Republican administrations invested in great projects that benefited everybody, from the workers who built them to the businesses that still use them today.

In the next few weeks, I will sign an executive order clearing away the red tape that slows down too many construction projects. But you need to fund these projects. Take the money we're no longer spending at war, use half of it to pay down our debt, and use the rest to do some nation-building right here at home.

(Applause.)

There's never been a better time to build, especially since the construction industry was one of the hardest hit when the housing bubble burst. Of course, construction workers weren't the only ones who were hurt. So were millions of innocent Americans who've seen their home values decline. And while government can't fix the problem on its own, responsible homeowners shouldn't have to sit and wait for the housing market to hit bottom to get some relief.

And that's why I'm sending this Congress a plan that gives every responsible homeowner the chance to save about

$3,000 a year on their mortgage, by refinancing at historically low rates.

(Applause.)

No more red tape. No more runaround from the banks. A small fee on the largest financial institutions will ensure that it won't add to the deficit and will give those banks that were rescued by taxpayers a chance to repay a deficit of trust. (Applause.)

Let's never forget: Millions of Americans who work hard and play by the rules every day deserve a government and a financial system that do the same. It's time to apply the same rules from top to bottom. No bailouts, no handouts, and no copouts. An America built to last insists on responsibility from everybody.

We've all paid the price for lenders who sold mortgages to people who couldn't afford them, and buyers who knew they couldn't afford them. That's why we need smart regulations to prevent irresponsible behavior.

(Applause.) Rules to prevent financial fraud or toxic dumping or faulty medical devices -- these don't destroy the free market. They make the free market work better.

There's no question that some regulations are outdated, unnecessary, or too costly. In fact, I've approved fewer regulations in the first three years of my presidency than my Republican predecessor did in his.

(Applause.)

I've ordered every federal agency to eliminate rules that don't make sense. We've already announced over 500 reforms, and just a fraction of them will save business and citizens more than $10 billion over the next five years. We got rid of one rule from 40 years ago that could have forced some dairy farmers to spend $10,000 a year proving that they could contain a spill -- because milk was somehow classified as an oil. With a rule like that, I guess it was worth crying over spilled milk.

(Now, I'm confident a farmer can contain a milk spill without a federal agency looking over his shoulder.

(Applause.)

Absolutely, but I will not back down from making sure an oil company can contain the kind of oil spill we saw in the Gulf two years ago.

(Applause.)

I will not back down from protecting our kids from mercury poisoning, or making sure that our food is safe and our water is clean. I will not go back to the days when health insurance companies had unchecked power to cancel your policy, deny your coverage, or charge women differently than men.

(Applause.)

And I will not go back to the days when Wall Street was allowed to play by its own set of rules. The new rules we passed restore what should be any financial system's core purpose: Getting funding to entrepreneurs with the best ideas, and getting loans to responsible families who want to buy a home, or start a business, or send their kids to college.

So if you are a big bank or financial institution, you're no longer allowed to make risky bets with your customers' deposits. You're required to write out a "living will" that details exactly how you'll pay the bills if you fail —- because the rest of us are not bailing you out ever again.

(Applause.)

And if you're a mortgage lender or a payday lender or a credit card company, the days of signing people up for products they can't afford with confusing forms and deceptive practices -- those days are over. Today, American consumers finally have a watchdog in Richard Cordray with one job: To look out for them.

(Applause.)

We'll also establish a Financial Crimes Unit of highly trained investigators to crack down on large-scale fraud and protect people's investments. Some financial firms violate major anti-fraud laws because there's no real penalty for being a repeat offender. That's bad for consumers, and it's bad for the vast majority of bankers and financial service professionals who do the right thing. So pass legislation that makes the penalties for fraud count.

And tonight, I'm asking my Attorney General to create a special unit of federal prosecutors and leading state attorney general to expand our investigations into the abusive lending and packaging of risky mortgages that led to the housing crisis.

(Applause.)

This new unit will hold accountable those who broke the law, speed assistance to homeowners, and help turn the page on an era of recklessness that hurt so many Americans.

Now, a return to the American values of fair play and shared responsibility will help protect our people and our economy. But it should also guide us as we look to pay down our debt and invest in our future.

Right now, our most immediate priority is stopping a tax hike on 160 million working Americans while the recovery is still fragile. (Applause.) People cannot afford losing $40 out of each paycheck this year. There are plenty of ways to get this done. So let's agree right here, right now: No side issues. No drama. Pass the payroll tax cut without delay. Let's get it done.

(Applause.)

When it comes to the deficit, we've already agreed to more than $2 trillion in cuts and savings. But we need to do more, and that means making choices. Right now, we're poised to spend nearly $1 trillion more on what was supposed to be a temporary tax break for the wealthiest 2 percent of Americans. Right now, because of loopholes and shelters in the tax code, a quarter of all millionaires pay lower tax rates than millions of middle-class households. Right now, Warren Buffett pays a lower tax rate than his secretary.

Do we want to keep these tax cuts for the wealthiest Americans? Or do we want to keep our investments in everything else –- like education and medical research; a strong military and care for our veterans? Because if we're serious about paying down our debt, we can't do both.

The American people know what the right choice is. So do I. As I told the Speaker this summer, I'm prepared to make more reforms that rein in the long-term costs of Medicare and Medicaid, and strengthen Social Security, so long as those programs remain a guarantee of security for seniors.

But in return, we need to change our tax code so that people like me, and an awful lot of members of Congress, pay our fair share of taxes.

(Applause.)

Tax reform should follow the Buffett Rule. If you make more than $1 million a year, you should not pay less than 30 percent in taxes. And my Republican friend Tom Coburn is right: Washington should stop subsidizing millionaires. In fact, if you're earning a million dollars a year, you shouldn't get special tax subsidies or deductions. On the other hand, if you make under $250,000 a year, like 98 percent of American families, your taxes shouldn't go up.

(Applause.)

You're the ones struggling with rising costs and stagnant wages. You're the ones who need relief.

Now, you can call this class warfare all you want. But asking a billionaire to pay at least as much as his secretary in taxes? Most Americans would call that common sense.

We don't begrudge financial success in this country. We admire it. When Americans talk about folks like me paying my fair share of taxes, it's not because they envy the rich. It's because they understand that when I get a tax break I don't need and the country can't afford, it either adds to the deficit, or somebody else has to make up the difference -- like a senior on a fixed income, or a student trying to get through school, or a family trying to make ends meet. That's not right. Americans know that's not right. They know that this generation's success is only possible because past generations felt a responsibility to each other, and to the future of their country, and they know our way of life will only endure if we feel that same sense of shared responsibility. That's how we'll reduce our deficit. That's an America built to last. (Applause.)

Now, I recognize that people watching tonight have differing views about taxes and debt, energy and health care. But no matter what party they belong to, I bet most Americans are thinking the same thing right about now: Nothing will get done in Washington this year, or next year, or maybe even the year after that, because Washington is broken.

Can you blame them for feeling a little cynical?

The greatest blow to our confidence in our economy last year didn't come from events beyond our control. It came from a debate in Washington over whether the United States would pay its bills or not. Who benefited from that fiasco?

I've talked tonight about the deficit of trust between Main Street and Wall Street. But the divide between this city and the rest of the country is at least as bad -- and it seems to get worse every year.

Some of this has to do with the corrosive influence of money in politics. So together, let's take some steps to fix that. Send me a bill that bans insider trading by members of

Congress; I will sign it tomorrow. (Applause.) Let's limit any elected official from owning stocks in industries they impact. Let's make sure people who bundle campaign contributions for Congress can't lobby Congress, and vice versa -- an idea that has bipartisan support, at least outside of Washington.

Some of what's broken has to do with the way Congress does its business these days. A simple majority is no longer enough to get anything -- even routine business -- passed through the Senate. (Applause.) Neither party has been blameless in these tactics. Now both parties should put an end to it. (Applause.) For starters, I ask the Senate to pass a simple rule that all judicial and public service nominations receive a simple up or down vote within 90 days.

(Applause.)

The executive branch also needs to change. Too often, it's inefficient, outdated and remote.

(Applause.)

That's why I've asked this Congress to grant me the authority to consolidate the federal bureaucracy, so that our government is leaner, quicker, and more responsive to the needs of the American people.

(Applause.)

Finally, none of this can happen unless we also lower the temperature in this town. We need to end the notion that the two parties must be locked in a perpetual campaign of mutual destruction; that politics is about clinging to rigid ideologies instead of building consensus around common-sense ideas.

I'm a Democrat. But I believe what Republican Abraham Lincoln believed: That government should do for people only what they cannot do better by themselves, and no more. (Applause.) That's why my education reform offers more competition, and more control for schools and states. That's why we're getting rid of regulations that don't work. That's why our health care law relies on a reformed private market, not a government program.

On the other hand, even my Republican friends who complain the most about government spending have supported federally financed roads, and clean energy projects, and federal offices for the folks back home.

The point is, we should all want a smarter, more effective government.   And while we may not be able to bridge our biggest philosophical differences this year, we can make real progress.   With or without this Congress, I will keep taking actions that help the economy grow.   But I can do a whole lot more with your help.   Because when we act together, there's nothing the United States of America can't achieve.

(Applause.)

That's the lesson we've learned from our actions abroad over the last few years.

Ending the Iraq war has allowed us to strike decisive blows against our enemies.   From Pakistan to Yemen, the al Qaeda operatives who remain are scrambling, knowing that they can't escape the reach of the United States of America.

(Applause.)

From this position of strength, we've begun to wind down the war in Afghanistan. Ten thousand of our troops have come home. Twenty-three thousand more will leave by the end of this summer. This transition to Afghan lead will continue, and we will build an enduring partnership with Afghanistan, so that it is never again a source of attacks against America. (Applause.)

As the tide of war recedes, a wave of change has washed across the Middle East and North Africa, from Tunis to Cairo; from Sana'a to Tripoli. A year ago, Qaddafi was one of the world's longest-serving dictators -– a murderer with American blood on his hands. Today, he is gone. And in Syria, I have no doubt that the Assad regime will soon discover that the forces of change cannot be reversed, and that human dignity cannot be denied.

(Applause.)

How this incredible transformation will end remains uncertain. But we have a huge stake in the outcome. And while it's ultimately up to the people of the region to decide their fate, we will advocate for those values that have served our own country so well. We will stand against violence and intimidation. We will stand for the rights and dignity of all human beings –- men and women; Christians, Muslims and Jews. We will support policies that lead to strong and stable democracies and open markets, because tyranny is no match for liberty.

And we will safeguard America's own security against those who threaten our citizens, our friends, and our interests. Look at Iran. Through the power of our diplomacy, a world that was once divided about how to deal with Iran's nuclear program now stands as one. The regime is more isolated than ever before; its leaders are faced with crippling sanctions, and as long as they shirk their responsibilities, this pressure will not relent.

Let there be no doubt: America is determined to prevent Iran from getting a nuclear weapon, and I will take no options off the table to achieve that goal.

(Applause.)

But a peaceful resolution of this issue is still possible, and far better, and if Iran changes course and meets its obligations, it can rejoin the community of nations.

The renewal of American leadership can be felt across the globe. Our oldest alliances in Europe and Asia are stronger than ever. Our ties to the Americas are deeper. Our ironclad commitment -- and I mean ironclad -- to Israel's security has meant the closest military cooperation between our two countries in history. (Applause.)

We've made it clear that America is a Pacific power, and a new beginning in Burma has lit a new hope. From the coalition's we've built to secure nuclear materials, to the missions we've led against hunger and disease; from the blows we've dealt to our enemies, to the enduring power of our moral example, America is back.

Anyone who tells you otherwise, anyone who tells you that America is in decline or that our influence has waned, doesn't know what they're talking about. (Applause.)

That's not the message we get from leaders around the world that are eager to work with us. That's not how people feel from Tokyo to Berlin, from Cape Town to Rio, where opinions of America are higher than they've been in years. Yes, the world is changing. No, we can't control every event. But America remains the one indispensable nation in world affairs –- and as long as I'm President, I intend to keep it that way. (Applause.)

That's why, working with our military leaders, I've proposed a new defense strategy that ensures we maintain the finest military in the world, while saving nearly half a trillion dollars in our budget. To stay one step ahead of our adversaries, I've already sent this Congress legislation that will secure our country from the growing dangers of cyber-threats.

(Applause.)

Above all, our freedom endures because of the men and women in uniform who defend it.

(Applause.)

As they come home, we must serve them as well as they've served us. That includes giving them the care and the benefits they have earned –- which is why we've increased annual VA spending every year I've been President.

(Applause.)

And it means enlisting our veterans in the work of rebuilding our nation.

With the bipartisan support of this Congress, we're providing new tax credits to companies that hire vets. Michelle and Jill Biden have worked with American businesses to secure a pledge of 135,000 jobs for veterans and their families. And tonight, I'm proposing a Veterans Jobs Corps that will help our communities hire veterans as cops and firefighters, so that America is as strong as those who defend her.

(Applause.)

Which brings me back to where I began? Those of us who've been sent here to serve can learn a thing or two from the service of our troops. When you put on that uniform, it doesn't matter if you're black or white; Asian, Latino, Native American; conservative, liberal; rich, poor; gay, straight. When you're marching into battle, you look out for the person next to you, or the mission fails. When you're in the thick of the fight, you rise or fall as one unit, serving one nation, leaving no one behind.

One of my proudest possessions is the flag that the SEAL Team took with them on the mission to get bin Laden. On it is each of their names. Some may be Democrats. Some may be Republicans. But that doesn't matter. Just like it didn't matter, that day in the Situation Room, when I sat next to Bob Gates -- a man who was George Bush's defense secretary -- and Hillary Clinton -- a woman who ran against me for president.

All that mattered that day was the mission. No one thought about politics. No one thought about themselves. One of the young men involved in the raid later told me that he didn't deserve credit for the mission. It only succeeded, he said, because every single member of that unit did their job -- the pilot who landed the helicopter that spun out of control; the translator who kept others from entering the compound; the troops who separated the women and children from the fight; the SEALs who charged up the stairs. More than that, the mission only succeeded because every member of that unit trusted each other -- because you can't charge up those stairs, into darkness and danger, unless you know that there's somebody behind you, watching your back.

So it is with America. Each time I look at that flag, I'm reminded that our destiny is stitched together like those 50 stars and those 13 stripes. No one built this country on their own. This nation is great because we built it together. This nation is great because we worked as a team. This nation is great because we get each other's backs. And if we hold fast to that truth, in this moment of trial, there is no challenge too great; no mission too hard. As long as we are joined in common purpose, as long as we maintain our common resolve, our journey moves forward, and our future is hopeful, and the state of our Union will always be strong.

Thank you, God Bless you, and God bless the United States of America.

(Applause.)

The United States of America first became debt free in 1835, which was probably the last time this greatest nation on earth was debt free

The President then was Andrew Jackson a Democrat.

FOUR

∞∞∞∞∞∞∞∞∞∞∞∞∞∞∞∞

THE PROMISES OF PRESIDENT OBAMA

The Road map to the United States of America presidential elections in November 2012 was written to enlighten the public on America's finest political debates, history, and how America has been able to excel in her brand of democracy which remains envious and encouraging to most nations. We will start with how President Obama became the winner of 2008 election and graduated it to 2012.

The Oracle was formerly not a friend nor was a supporter of President Barack Obama until 2008, Hillary Clinton the preferred choice of the Oracle due to former

President Bill Clinton's pedigree and commendable performances in office. It had thought that President Clinton would hand over power to his wife once she was able to secure nomination for presidency by the Democratic Party.

Senator Barack Obama was perceived as a rookie, a first time Senator who would just grace the primaries like all the blacks before him e.g. Reverend Jesse Jackson of Rainbow Collation fame and Reverend Al Sharpton a political commentator on MSNBC network.

However, the Harvard Law Professor with strong root from the Luo Tribe in Kenya in Africa was different.

Senator Barack Obama, a sharp, intelligent, smart and an amiable personality, a fine looking tall black man with graceful smiles was able to convince many difficult voters with his powerful speeches and sincerity of purpose. The Oracle, like any other American with Clintonian hangover, never paid any serious attention to Senator Obama. It had thought that history was going to represent itself, and that was going to be the year for the emergence of America's first woman President!

Supporters of Hillary had listened to the campaign song Céline Dion's "High on the mountain", while, the supporters of Bill Clinton were sending money and affections to facilitate Hillary's nomination at the primaries. To us, Senator Barack Obama and his ambition would soon fade away and we would be back to what we did in the past; picking our candidates from the traditional packs of the White candidates. That was the history we knew, it was not going to change, may be not in our generation, so we thought!

In the state of Texas, Dallas City, the home town to most America's Fortune 500 hundred companies, only three things were important aside business. "The Cowboys football team", called America's team; it was indeed the best team. "The Mavericks", the basketball team which a billionaire Mark Cuba bought and was expected to be the America's Team like the Cowboys, and Fox News Channel, a conservative news in every home that was the media established to check the influences of the Liberal controlled MSNBC or CNN in the State. As for the Fox News Channels, nothing could be good about the Democrats, while the television channel presented President George Bush, like one of the characters described in "Julius Caesar Shakespeare" a saint who could never be wrong!

Texas State is the heartbeat of the Republican Party, the strong nerve of capitalism and indeed the center of white man control of United States economy. The state of Texas alone represents 35 to 40 percent of United States of America exports. If you remove Texas as a State from America and make it a country, it will be 13th richest country on the face of the earth!

Texas is rich in oil and human resources, it contains all the three M's of business, money, men and materials and the 4 P's of marketing Price, Products, Promotion and Placement. It implies that the state has the capability to remove unwanted product in business or determine a candidate for any election.

The State of Texas has about 15 percent African Americans and 25 percent Hispanics, is expected to increase to 35percent in future because the Hispanics have tendencies to bear more babies than any other groups in America; A comedian once said, in El Paso Texas, "if you don't want kids, please don't date a Mexican lady, because they don't use birth control pills, they are mostly Catholics or Christians".

The rest of her populations are whites or Caucasians from every nooks and crannies of the State. Republican Party is seen as the party of choice in Texas. In spite of this, it never affected the growth of Democratic Party which had started losing its grip on the State since President Lyndon B. Johnson signed the civil rights bill.

From history, when President Abraham Lincoln freed the slaves, Texas State waited for five years before she announced the freedom of the African Americans. In spite of the freedom given, it is still a conservative State and very evangelical. Any observer with a third eye could feel the pain in the hearts of the whites and the blacks; the trust is still not as strong as one would have expected. In Texas, people still sit separately at lunch-time according to race. An immigrant would be left confused to see them again working together in the same office.

How has it influenced the choice of candidates for the Office of the President? How has Senator Barack Obama with his root in Africa and White Mother from Kansas State be able to charm his way into the hearts of Americans? Senator Obama was not ordinarily expected to win the Democratic Party primaries or the Presidency because of the small population of the Blacks or African Americans. All he needed was just a magic wand to propel him to the lime light in the manner of his African American predecessors.

Until FOX Channel News, a conservative media, with locations all over the nation, made the greatest mistake ever; it went after Senator Obama's Pastor raising racial issues which became national concern under reference.

This news was first cast by Sean Hannity. When race became a national issue, Senator Obama from the State of Illinois was compelled to address the National Press on a prime time televised all over America.

During the presentation, Barack Obama displayed the candor of a professorial enlightenment distinct from any Black man ever in the national limelight ever since the time of Rev. Martin Luther King Jr. He enlightened a confused nation on the issue of race. He traced the history of the American constitution which was written in City of Philadelphia which did not fully address the issue of equality, in the speech he titled "Towards a Perfect Union".

His presentations drew tears from the eyes of every hard stone believer of the Clintons, it softened the minds of the conservatives, it captured the independent voters, it pulled the youths behind him and for the first time, race became a secondary issue and America was one country with a common goal; then the Oracle switched to Obama.

When Senator Obama was reminded that he wanted to reap from where he did not sow, because his father was not born in America, he addressed the issue with another heart compelling words of unity.

"I stand on the shoulders of Giant" he gave tributes to past leaders like Dr. Martin Luther King Jr. Malcolm X, Rev. Jesse Jackson and Rev. Al Sharpton. He had his African American supporter base,   which had also supported President Clinton to remain neutral. The first "Black Berry" candidate in American history was set to sweep the election. Eventually, Hillary Clinton accepted Obama's candidature as the Democrat Party nominee as he was set to challenge the "Old man" and US Senate veteran Senator John McCain from Arizona State for the November Presidential elections.

A Republican from Texas reminded the voters of Republican Party's contributions to the Blacks Freedom during President Abraham Lincoln's presidency. With the Oracle's African background, he believed this wisdom of Africans- "when you give a dog to a man, you don't keep the leash".

This means if President Abraham Lincoln or the Republican Party truly freed the slaves, why did he not give absolute right to vote and be elected at that same time?

It should be assumed that a political party that gave the right to vote gave absolute freedom to the blacks in America as citizens. This is the thrust of most blacks and African Americans belief and choice as Democrats.

Midway into the campaigns by both Senator Obama and Senator John McCain, public opinion had shifted to the side of Senator Barack Obama because the economy of America was crumbling and several thousands were losing their jobs and life savings.

When it became obvious that the Republicans were losing reputation fast, John Kayman a Republican friend from the state of Texas, gave seven reasons why citizens should cast their votes for his Party. However, this Oracle gave seventeen reasons why he would rather pitch tent with the Democrat.

The rest is now history. America, for the first time in the history of the nation, 40 years after the prediction of late Robert Kennedy who was killed in 1968, and 43 years after the civil right bill was signed, elected the first Black or half Black President. The country was happy at the result and the whole world was happy for America.

Has President Obama delivered on the promises he made before elections? How has he fared? Has he performed as expected?

Does he deserve to be re-elected the second term? Or one term will be all he would get from a nation that has never had a President of different color until now?

The Oracle will also take a look at Mitt Romney and his monies and how that may affect his chances for the presidential bid.

Those who grew up in Africa, at the time the economy of Nigeria-the richest Black country collapsed, during the rule of the maximum dictator, General Sanni Abacha, the Military Head of State, would understand better the situation in

America. That was the worst economic plunge in Africa's largest concentration of black race. Most of the working capital and lifesavings disappeared from the Banking and financial institutions including Forum finance House which held quite substantial public and private funds.

Companies closed down, fear became the future of the country and the people, more so, when there was nothing like bail-out for the economy. Government opinion was to allow the market forces to take care of the situation.

The military government assured the nation that the situation would be alright, it never did. Manufacturing industries closed down along with banks and financial institutions. There were no credit facilities again to cushion the economy. That became the end for most businesses that had to close shops. This downturn was also the beginning of the events that changed the lives of over 150 million people in the south of Sahara. Most Nigerians left the country en mass by road, air land and sea on a journey most of them never returned.

The world most powerful nation, America was on the verge of similar situation, before Senator Barack Obama became the 44th President. The former President Bush was leaving behind a system that had crippled the economy of United States of America because of the two wars. The funding of the wars in Iraq and Afghanistan dwindled the economy resulting in a deficit of almost three billion dollars weekly.

The America's power house, the Middle class had virtually been destroyed with a monthly 750 thousands job loss. Most of the financial institutions closed down for lack of funds and patronage. The mortgage or housing industry collapsed, manufacturing industries, particularly the auto section had nothing more to offer and most cities became empty as people walked away from their properties because they could not afford mortgage.

Detroit, in the state of Michigan became the hardest hit in the crisis, with over 1.2 million populations which were subsequently reduced to 750 thousand. There was mass exodus from the Motor City for lack of jobs. Banking and financial institutions were greatly affected with the crash in housing, stocks and financial instruments. It was the greatest problem ever inherited by a President since 1945.

United States of America, the doyen of capitalism and the hope of self-actualization on what you can dream of became a country in fear. Some people wanted the President George Bush to leave before his term expired; they believed he had lost touch with the reality on how to save the economy from crisis.

However, what the incoming President could offer a troubled nation was, his reassuring smiles, Harvard University coolness to issues, radiance of confidence given his unmatched diversity of his background which put him as African, Asian and Caucasian; his paternal Muslim background, from the Luo tribe in African continent all wrapped together in one package. Yet inside the nation was the fear of the Middle Class destroyed, with the unfavorable policies of the outgoing

President Bush on the economic policies that favored the Rich alone.

What will be future of the country and the hope of the nation in the world politics?

Will Capitalism end like the Soviet Union's socialism? Will the country be reduced to the third world nation like it happened during the Forum Finance House era of General Sanni Abacha? Will the new President save the nation from glaring economic problems ahead?

There was a popular movie in those days called "Other People's Money" by Danny DeVito such was the system of America economy; the Wall Street lives on the investments of every nation and the largeness of the Banking industry was transferred to all the sectors of the economy.

By the time President Bush left office, the Islamic world had lost interest in United States America economy, they emptied the banks and there was no credit facility to keep the country going again, with the two wars, and a tax free system for the rich, the government had no revenue to keep the system going than to borrow from friends and enemies, China a friend and economic competitor of America doctored its currency in exchange for loan to the country.

The new President went to work; he had to normalize the relationship with the Arab World which was messed up by President Bush. He appointed former Senator Hillary Clinton as his Secretary of State and both became the best America could offer the world to reset the button of friendship.

However, the Republicans did not approve the change of plan from war to friendship, but the President persisted some said, he bowed for the King of Saudi Arabia, the President said he respected the custom of other nations.

He held Town Hall meetings in Turkey and Egypt and the citizens of most Muslim countries for the first time were able to ask the questions they had never asked any American President before him. As a result, President Obama became friendlier to these nations than the former President George Bush from Crawford, Texas.

The Muslim world, though reluctant to accept hands of friendship of America's new President, however, appreciate President Obama's friendly disposition and counted him worthy of their trust again, more than President Bill Clinton or President Jimmy Carter. In fact, most third world nations trusted American leadership under Democrats more than the Republicans.

At home, the President took care of the minimum wage of the workers from $5.25 to $7.25 which was last increased, when President Bill Clinton was in office. He approved the funding of sperm cell that was closed down by President Bush, he corrected all the problems put in the middle class, supported the economy with a new bailout to cushion the pain pending the restoration of confidence in the banking industry.

President Obama's government bailed out the Auto industries from the financial stress. The crises had relieved almost 1.7 million people from work. Years later, the result became glaring as America is now the world's best Auto industry again. Repositioning American economy has turned his hair grey in a short while!

While the Republicans wanted the market forces to take care of the economy, on issues of bankruptcy or unemployment; which would have destroyed the middle class; however, the President upheld his belief in the plight of an average American, and especially the poor.

At the time the GOP enjoyed President Bush tax free era for the Rich, many of the beneficiaries placed their investments in Cayman Island and Swiss banks while most American companies like Halliburton moved their corporate office overseas where they sourced jobs overseas from countries like India and Asia.

Furthermore, average jobs like customer service, and call centers were also transferred overseas by these companies which enjoyed President Bush tax free system for the Rich. This was to avoid helping the new administration create jobs locally.

If the Bush tax cut which expired in 2010 was discontinued, it would have added over one trillion dollars as revenue to the government. However, the Republicans controlled Congress disallowed it, threatening to block unemployment benefits to the poor in the country if President Obama failed to extend Bush Tax policy.

The President consented and extended the Bush tax cut for the Rich if the poor would be allowed to keep their unemployment benefit. His supporter base the Liberal was not happy. They felt he should have stood his ground on the Tax free system to the Rich.

However, the Harvard Professor of Law knew better, that this could become an election issue in November; also the crime rate would have gone up more if he had not.

When British Petroleum Company messed up the Costal states with oil spillage, President Obama handled the problem without spending a cent from the national purse. He reorganized the FEMA and other government agencies and spent more than his predecessors for the veterans with improvement on warrior transition programs for soldiers and their benefits.

On foreign affairs, he performed better than his predecessor. Osama Bin Laden who masterminded the September 11th attack that caused the death of almost 3000 people in New York was killed by the Navy Seal. This decision was taken though his top advisers and the Secretary of State had thought otherwise.

President Obama's government encouraged internal revolution to prevail in countries with dictators, like Libya, Syria, Egypt, and Algeria which was cheaper for America, unlike the Republicans that wanted another war with these nations.

Interestingly, when it was time to ask the Americans for his second term bid in November 2012, he did it first, with a song of Al Green which he sang with a big smile at the Apollo Theater in Harlem New York recently. It was titled "I am so in love with you"; the questions for the Americans will be if the love is real or not?

Will the same love be given to the Republicans or President Barack Obama for another term in November elections?

From all indications, the man with his wealth hidden in Cayman Island, and Swiss Bank is likely to represent the Republicans in November elections. At a time the Americans were coming out of economic mess with job increase to almost new 250 thousands per month since 2005, and the recovery of the manufacturing industry. Former Governor Mitt Romney, once said, he loved firing people, he would therefore not be concerned with the loss of mortgage.

Will Gov. Mitt Romney win the love of the nation, and therefore discontinue with Obama Medicare and other agencies like Consumer Affairs, ecological and environment or too big to fail system, created to save the economy and improve the system?

As predicted by the Oracle, the average American, the poor and middle class will remember President Obama as a friend who stood by them when they were down; who gave a helping hand when they lost their houses; and when they were sick with all the programs created by former President Bush which almost destroyed the middle class, he bailed them out.

The Oracle says, this is the future of America, President Obama will be back in Office with more than 53.3 percent majority and most of the swing or battle states will find comfort with the policies of President Obama which will kick in over 40 million new beneficiaries of Affordable Health care Act and the Republicans will be left gasping, wondering at the smartness of the man from Harvard University and master of Chicago politics.

Like Oliver Twist, the country wants more from President Obama, normally, it takes some time to rebuild, though, it is easier to destroy. This is the wisdom in patience the President is demanding from his people if he secures his second term like President Clinton.

America will witness economic boom like the Clinton era again. The set target will be the creation of 30 million new jobs. This figure is above President Clinton 22 million jobs created but if President Obama fails to secure his second term bid, all the gains of the past will be rolled back and the middle class may be negatively affected.

However, the Oracle will like to assure its readers that there is no vacancy in the White House as the GOP had thought, by November elections. Perhaps what makes America politics very interesting and distinguished from all other democratic practices around the world, is the expanded primary system which the country administers to select or nominate a candidate for the highest office in the country.

This system gives all Americans the opportunity to now assess the candidates well. It exposes their shortcomings and therefore present voters with options for the elimination of unprepared candidates before the party choice of its flag bearer at the convention.

The expanded primaries also help to destroy multiple party systems operating in most third world nations. For anyone who wants to understand the beauty of America democratic structure this is it.

Following this practice, America has been able to merge all ideologies into two formidable political parties without destroying others, which are reduced to pressure groups within the system. For a long time to come, America will be governed by either the Democrats or the Republican Party, in spite the existence of Green Party, Tea Party and Lutheran Party which may all find a place within the two formidable parties.

In the course of these contests, it is the practice to organize political debates by television stations like CNN, MSBC, Fox New, ABC, CBS etc. this is an avenue where difficult questions are answered to convincingly to determine the most qualified contestant for the highest office earning $400 thousand dollars remuneration.

This is the procedure each contestant must follow at the State primary elections to secure votes before the convention in the July or August in Tampa Florida State. This usually takes four months before the general election.

The Oracle will review the Republican Party's activities in this article. It started with about eight candidates; including Congress woman Michelle Bachman who later found out that America was not prepared for a female President under the GOP, unlike the Democratic Party which almost nominated Senator Hillary Clinton four years ago.

Somehow, the Congress woman found herself defending a program she earlier opposed with some of the dealings of her husband who had benefitted from the program she was campaigning against. By the time she dropped out in January 2012, it was not a surprise to the average American.

In America, a politician could be forgiven for many things, from adultery to substance abuse etc. however, the country abhors liars, a dishonest person is perceived as a vomit, and he or she could be blown off like the candle light. Americans, following the experience of former President Bush, are skillful in shifting responses to inquiries and could discern dislikes from questions answered during interviews. Governor of Texas Rick Perry was blown off his feet during contest like the wind in the desert land of El Paso; he could not remember the answer to his own question taken from his own book.

When Chris Matthew the MSNBC coordinator of Hardball program said, the Governor of Texas did not have enough brain to be President of America, all the flames and support the Governor of Texas had from the evangelicals and conservatives evaporated like a cup of water in the sun. The Oracle had the opportunity of meeting the Governor about four years ago, in Austin Texas, somehow, believed, Rick Perry was more of a clone of former President Bush with his gesticulations. Bearing the former President's economic record and overspending drifts, Americans would not want to go through that Texas route again; this made Rick Perry guilty by association.

The Oracle predicted in October 2011 that Governor Rick Perry would drop out of the race before February 2012. Interestingly, he dropped out when all he could get was less than six percent in most of the returns of the elections in the States of New Hampshire, IOWA; leaving the stage to Speaker Newt Gingrich and Rick Santorum, Mitt Romney and Dr. Ron Paul of Texas.

The Florida State primary result kept the former Speaker Newt Gingrich away from limelight after he was reduced to a grouchy old man due to the financial muscle of Mitt Romney and GOP presidential nomination. It is now a contest between former Senator Rick Santorum and Mitt Romney when Dr. Ron Paul is expected to drop out of the race before April 2nd 2012.

Sadly Newt Gingrich has limited time due to his age; there may never be another opportunity for him, if he fails to secure nomination this year, which is doubtful. Apparently, he may be left behind with his proposal for "America's 51st State in the Moon" which made him a joker to the electorates.

However, as the America economy improves, the vacancy signpost in the White House is gradually being removed, more so with the public opinion in favor of

President Barack Obama. The Republicans are left confused; they have no convincing message for the Americans except cultural war, religion and contraception.

Interestingly, in the GOP, you observe men fighting on behalf of women, as if, they carry pregnancies. This is another "Aspirin technology" battle fought between their legs one of the bankers to Rick Santorum mention on national television.

Joe Scarborough of the MSNBC, said years ago, that "to find a lead actor for a movie, you have to write the script first" the Republicans could not write a convincing script hence, they could not make up their minds on Rick Santorum or the money man Governor Mitt Romney.

To the Republicans, despite the fact that, Governor Mitt Romney would sometimes wear jeans to make him look like a regular guy on the street, the Americans still looked beyond the jeans and all they could see is a nice Tuxedo suite full of money of various currencies, like Japanese Yen, Pounds, and probably Naira. A business man who loves to fire people, and insensitive man who said, he does not care for the poor with all his wealth locked away in Cayman Island and Swiss Banks. He may probably be the richest to ever run for the office of the President. America despite her love of money, may still find it difficult to completely trust and accept this businessman from the State of Michigan.

Interestingly, this will be Mitt Romney second time around, he is name all over the country, not as a defender of the middle class, but as the representative of the one percent class that pay lesser in tax than an average American. When compared to President Obama, Governor Mitt Romney and his past records look like a Jacob wearing the suit of Esau i.e. a Democrat in Republican outfit.

Public opinion, when considered, most likely would favor the candidate who identified and sympathized with the middle class. This candidate may eventually become the President.

Moreover, Senator Rick Santorum, as predicted weeks ago by the Oracle looks promising and may be the true representative of the conservatives and the evangelicals. Of recent, he received the evangelical backing in Texas. His life style embodies all attributes of a true Republican party; married with seven children; he never believed in birth Control; his ideology appears old fashion for his age at 53. Despite his good looks, he talked like a man still in the 20th Century which is the general view and value system of the GOP. Just like the former President George Bush said, in his program of education, Rick Santorum may be the "Child left Behind" by the new development around him in the 21st Century; and the gains of America in the last 50 years like civil rights, women's right to choose, and internet age.

The assumed GOP nominee for the November election will emerge in the next three weeks which the system refers to as "Super Tuesday," in when most States will hold their primaries. The Oracle, believes that should the GOP still holds on deeply to their policies on abortion, religion and unfriendly immigration policies, Rick Santorum will emerge as the candidate. However, should they fail to win in November, 2012, the Party holds the blame and not the candidate for the

20th Century ideas. If the objective is definite on winning election, Governor Mitt Romney will be the candidate of the Party. This means, that with his nomination, the Party has moved towards the Center of the conservative, it has embraced Mormon as a Christian, it has accepted part of Obama Care program; which may be a bit difficult for the average Republicans, this reality again makes President Barack Obama's Chicago politics unbeatable.

Finally, as the issue of contraception for women, improvement of the United States of America economy with job growth, and reduction in unemployment become the main issues of the debates in months to come, Oracle boldly predicts, this year will be the worst outings for the Republican Party and may not be as bad as a replay of how late President Reagan won by landslide victory during his second term.

Like the Oracle advised three years ago, the GOP must re-organize itself to understand the challenges of the 21st century. The Party must be inclusive in sex, race and ideas that will accommodate others like the gays rights, immigration tolerance and abortion i.e. the Party must in color, in deeds and ideas look like a true American Party not a white dominated Party or Christians alone, otherwise, the GOP may be out of office for the next sixteen years.

Again, the Oracle says there is no vacancy in the White House this year, for whoever is nominated by the GOP. President Barack Obama will be elected with more than 53.3 percent of the Electoral College or a figure more than 270 Electoral College. If Obama implements all his programs in Obama care and consumer watch dog activities in the next four years with a target of 30 million new jobs, GOP may become unpopular for a very long time to come.

Before Andrew Jackson became the President of America, he was a land speculator, in the state of Tennessee he learned to handle debt when a land deal went bad, and left him with massive debt and some worthless paper notes. When he became the President he knew his enemy, Banks and the national debt; "National debt is a curse, a moral failure and the ideal of acquiring stuff through debt almost seemed like black magic."

H Brand (Author of Biography of Andrew Jackson)

FIVE

∞∞∞∞∞∞∞∞∞∞∞∞∞∞

TIME TO TALK TO CREDITORS

The national debts of the United States of America that started like a joke under President Ronald Reagan in the eighties from 700 billion dollars being the accumulated debts arising from the Vietnam and the Second world wars, went up to 3.7 trillion by the time Reagan, the favorite of the Republicans left office equally, his successor President George H Bush, left office, hiked the national debt to a staggering figure of almost 8.7 trillion dollars.

However, during the economic boom of the nineties, the United States of America under President Bill Clinton created over 22 million new jobs and reduced the national debt to five trillion dollars. This feat made him the only President in American history that has made effort to reduce drastically, the national debt since President Andrew Jackson in 1837, the founder of the Democrat party.

When President George W Bush, took office, just like his father, President George H Bush, he also increased the debt to almost 11.7 trillion dollars at the end of his term. These debt problems, as well as the problem of failed economy were the critical issues that the new President had to contend with at the inception of his era.

President Obama bailed out several sectors to restored the economy; his critics said that he was not doing enough on a debt that attracts 1.8 trillion dollars interest. The fact remain obvious, even if the presidency does, and just focus on managing the debt alone, the United States national debt will still attract a minimum of 1.8 trillion on interest yearly.

What can he do? The only source of generating money for payment of the national debt locally without borrowing from friends and enemies is to let part of the Bush Tax policies introduced about ten years ago expire, i.e. to tax the Rich. A proposal rejected by the Republican controlled Congress; other option available to the President is to cut the defense budget which takes more than 40% of the US budget to relieve the economy however, this will affect the ego of the military and future gains of protracted wars abroad and American military might.

Maybe it is time to do what Nigerian government did during former President Olusegun Obasanjo tenure. In the nineties, his government was confronted with huge accumulated debt situation; he entered into negotiations with the creditors mainly the Paris and London Clubs and negotiated the repayment of the Principal debt, pleading for the write off the accumulated interest which the country may find highly unlikely to pay. With subtle diplomacy of the leadership at that time, the creditors agreed to the terms and his country became debt free.

In similar situation, we all do talk to our credit card companies for negotiation, it is time for the United States of America to talk to Japan, China, India and others to renegotiate the terms, a leeway to get off the interests and repayment of the Principal. Will this approach not affect the credit rating of the country?

The yearly interest payment of 1.8 trillion is sufficient enough to keep the US economy and the people in bondage. Added to, the burden of taxes paid by both the Rich and the Poor. However, if the nation agrees not to tax the Rich because it will affect the economy, the next and reliable option is to adapt the "Talk to the creditor approach".

It is advisable that USA adopts similar method; otherwise, in the next three years the national debt could be up to 20 trillion dollars with spiraling interest accruing to it. This is the bitter truth; it is time to talk to the creditors for a new deal.

We may not totally blame President Obama on how the economy is being managed; 1.8 trillion dollars interest without the principal is enough to paralyze the system. USA needs to sit down to renegotiate the terms with the creditors with a view to settle the principal. Each of the past leaders has been running the system like a credit card except President Clinton, will that be the approach of President Obama in his second term or find a better route on how to protect capitalism?

Maybe it is time to enter into discussion with China and Japan to moderate the loan package which is now very harsh and needed a review. President Obama will have to examine the future implications of his actions or inactions in a global economic war, which is being destroyed by the introduction of internet, which made outsourcing of America lost jobs to India, China and other nations, very easy and economical.

The first option recommended that the government of the United States of America must review the current interest rates to have a relief, and also find a way to get out of the imbroglio by taxing the rich; a decision the Republicans rejected abi initio, however, If the debt limit is increased by President Obama's Administration, it will be the 79th time since the time of the Republican President Dwight D. Eisenhower. (Less than 28 times under the Democrats Presidents, five times under Clinton, eight under President Bush and only once by Obama if eventually passed by the Congress.

The question is not even about the increase, it is about paying back the debt itself. Will the interest payment allow the government to meet its obligations like, social security, Medicare, Medicaid, defense industry, payment of contractors and other social and economic power services of the nation in the future?

These are the political and economic implications of the mounting debts on the economy of the free world. What are the financial implications of non-payment or default?

The President says the Triple A card or the gold card of United States credit rating will be affected. Like this writer wrote in the past, one of the reasons President Obama must be commended for saving the economy with the bail out of the Banking Industry is based on one single fact - US banking industry is like the Federal Reserve's Bank for the world, allowing it to collapse will spread the problem worldwide. That was what Obama's administration averted. Indeed, history will accord him the Hero of Capitalism of the 21st Century.

Internet has not only improved the world's economy, it has provided a complete leverage for all nations to operate on a level playing field of interests, where only the best will emerge winner. Today, most of the jobs that could have sustained the lower class of the economy have been taken away by this "internet monsters"; for example: customer service, help desk, or call centers.

The United States companies that wanted almost tax free system are not helping the system by shipping these jobs overseas, while technology continues to wipe away traditional jobs like typesetting etc. for most of them on computer, making the workers without tools of the future unwanted in a job hunt market which be the reason President Obama insisting on the policy of re-education for the American workers to meet the challenges ahead.

If America fails to talk to the Creditors, to review the interest rate, it is not only the credit rating that will be affected. It is the future of the coming generations; on a debt they could neither explain nor have something to gain.

Again, this ORACLE will like to plead with the government and all the stakeholders to open up a channel for review of the interest rates for the sake of the future generation. It is the wisest thing among all other options; the current approach is like a bridge to nowhere; the real issue is the interest and re-payment that is shifting to the unborn generation. It is not fair on them. Today, the average American share of the debt is almost $43K per person, and may grow to become $55K by December 2011.

'Whatever you did for one of the least of these brothers of mine, you did for me.'

(Verse 40)

Jesus Christ
Parable of the Sheep and Goats
Matthew 25:31-46

SIX

∞∞∞∞∞∞∞∞∞∞∞∞∞∞∞

FACTS AND MYTHS OF AFFORDABLE HEALTH CARE ACT

Five Important numbers from the new Obama care Affordable Health care Reforms Act

1.   54 million Americans now have coverage for preventive services free of charge as insurers are now required to cover a number of recommended preventives services such as cancer, diabetes, and blood pressure screening without additional cost sharing such as copays or deductibles

2.   32.5 million Americans with Medicare who need a free preventive service the new health reforms law eliminated a deductibles and copays for any preventable services or for a new annual wellness visit as a result of this new law over 20 million American seniors received a cardiovascular screening free of charge.

3.   3.6 million American Seniors saved over $2.1 billion on their prescription drugs an average of $600 for every senior who hit the cap in Medicare's prescription drug coverage often called "donut hole"

4.   2.5 million or more young adults have health insurance through their parent plan, under these health care reforms, most young adult who can't get coverage at work can stay on their parent coverage till the age of 26.

5.   50 thousands Americans with pre-existing conditions have gained coverage.

SEVEN

∞∞∞∞∞∞∞∞∞∞∞∞∞∞∞

WHY AMERICA CAN'T AFFORD MITT ROMNEY

POLICIES NOW?

An adage says, if you don't get what you want, you should like what is thrown at you otherwise you miss an opportunity. When the former Governor of Massachusetts, Mitt Romney won the Republican Party nomination with the delegates from the State of Texas, there was a change of heart for the conservatives, or the evangelicals. In the word of Chris Matthew, the anchor of the Hard Ball program of the MSNBC, the "Defenders of the status quo"; those who never wanted any change for the minority are those who would rather see

America operate like the time the minorities and the middle class never had any recognition in a country that graciously opened its doors to all races in the world.

The Oracle wrote a few months ago, that for the core base of the Republican Party or the Tea Party to vote for Mitt Romney, they will have to do two things not minding the values they stood for in the past. Firstly, they have to close their eyes, and secondly, cover their nose, then cast their vote for the man they don't really love. If Mitt Romney decides to replay his record in the state of Massachusetts as a Governor, it will be the same side of a coin.

When the Republicans particularly the Tea Party or the conservatives disliked President Obama for any reasons whatsoever, either for getting rid of Osama Bin laden on time a feat which the Former President George Bush could not perform throughout his eight years in office, or his birth certificate from the state of Hawaii, the last to join the Union, even for his diplomatic war strategies on Iran and North Korea including his evolving policy on the LBGT right to marry, the

Republicans could not but appreciate President Obama systematic and less expensive approach to domestic and international politics. Sadly, this is the situation the evangelicals and conservatives have found themselves; accept Mitt Romney with his shortcomings or allow President Obama to have a second term.

However, what happens to the evangelical principles of how a true Christian is measured following the comment from the Southern Christians on classification Mormon faith as a cult, or the moral lesson on how he has been unwilling to release details of his taxes for ten years at a time the banking industry collapsed under a Republican leadership in 2008 before President Obama took Office?

Today, Mitt Romney may be seen as a "saint" who may be the "Messiah" for the evangelicals and in spite of his past; of not being a perfect Christian will be overlooked. As is written in the Bible, when you become a "born again" all your sins will be forgotten and you will become "new" meaning, the conservatives will have to embrace him like the prodigal son or stay at home in November Presidential Elections. Will they?

Do they have a choice after the abortive presidential journeys of Governor Rick Perry of Texas, the fast talking former Senator Rick Santorum or the "Moon President" former Speaker Newt Gingrich became a big blow to the conservatives?

Are the conservatives shrinking in membership? The choice of Mitt Romney is the best that can happen to the Republican Party to get the middle class vote but how to get the votes of women, blacks and Latino will be a hard nut to crack, because of the record of President Obama who stood with the American workers as against the policies of the Republican Party.

Governor Mitt Romney will be too afraid to run on his record of the State of Massachusetts where he became the Apostle or fore runner of Obamacare, even his business knowledge with the Bain will likely not make him a good or trusted friend of American Middle Class.

President Obama, a former professor of the law of prestigious Harvard University was very practical in his definition of the job of the President. He took his audience on the memory lane on how past and successful leadership saw the governance of the country exclusively on people oriented values rather than by managing investment at a profit alone. It will be therefore be inadequate to rate presidential requirement by only 20 percent job capacity of the ability of Mitt Romney instead of looking at the core value, that leadership is all about the people.

It was Professor Peter Drucker of Canada, one of the Oracle's favorite management writers, who defined management as the ability to manage man, material and money, and when the opportunity is not available, the entrepreneur must create one. In his book "Management in the Turbulent Period" profit alone must not be regarded as the reasons for being in business. Later in his years, he expanded his theory to include power and politics. Sadly, this is the basis of Mitt Romney style, which is far from the reality in the free world.

The Oracle believes that government should be entirely about the people; this supports the definition of democracy as the government of the people, by the people, for the people, and not for the money or the top one percent in the society. When this dogma is removed from the definition of the government, the middle class will suffer and the bridge that creates an egalitarian society may be destroyed.

A true government of the people, must exist to create a level playing ground for all, it must hold the big hammer or the big stick to correct, when things are not going well without affecting the freedom and rights of the people. The government must never abandon the people at the expense of profit, or dump into the hostile hand of market forces. Above all, government must make the citizens welfare the center of its program. These are the values the Democrats in the United States of America upholds and is able to stand by the people when the tide turns; create opportunities like student loan, housing loan, Medicare, Medicaid, social security during old age, and to offer a helping hand when economy becomes unfavorable, a level ground for all in a country where everyone does his or her own fair share by operating carrot and stick value system, all of these, the Republicans fail to understand.

These are the values that sustain the American dream, the middle class and it is that which separates America from all other of the earth. America cannot afford to discard her functional value system that protects the middle class for the sake of market forces and the greedy eyes of the top one percent, these values are corroborated in the Holy Book, the Bible Matthew 25:35-40, probably what made President Andrew Jackson the founder of the Democratic Party a friend of the poor, the sick and workers upon which every president the party had given the country since 1837 took its values and principles.

The above, analysis is the Democrats perception of how a government must function. Regrettably, this is what a Mitt Romney Presidency may stand against, meaning that all the gains of the middle class will be eliminated: from student loans, freedom, right of women on their body, rights of the minorities and future of immigrants and elimination of labor unions which serves as a check on executive lawlessness of the states.

The understanding of the responsibility of the office of presidency in the mind of Governor Mitt Romney, may be that government must cut most programs that protect the middle class, the programs that reduce the rights of women, students loans and gains of the past 50 years all which protects the minorities and immigrants, and all policies that make America a melting ground for the immigrants which came from all over the world.

What will happen to all the programs that keep America's middle class robust if Mitt Romney wins the Presidency in 2012?

When I think about those Soldiers or Airmen or Marines or Sailors who are out there fighting on my behalf and yet feel constrained, even now that Don't Ask Don't Tell is gone, because they are not able to commit themselves in a marriage, at a certain point I've just concluded that for me personally it is important for me to go ahead and affirm that I think same sex couples should be able to get married.

President Barack Obama

EIGHT

∞∞∞∞∞∞∞∞∞∞∞∞∞∞

PRESIDENT OBAMA AND MARRIAGE
EQUALITY

When the anchor of Meet the Press David Gregory of MSNBC asked the vice President of the United States of America, Joe Biden views on gays right to marry like every other group that fought for equality and recognition in the last 125 years in the history of America, (Women's right to vote, blacks or African Americans civil rights of 1964; Indian Civil Rights Acts 1968; Marriage equality between whites and blacks, though not recognized by most states in America until

1968, and many more including the rights of women to choose (1973) in Roe Vs. Wade) , the Oracle was on his knees praying for guidance on the right response to the question from the anchor: political correspondent to the Liberal MSNBC who had on several occasions made a mockery of the White House late Press Secretary Mr. Tony Snow.

Vice President Joe Biden's reply made a statement that changed history and even the presidency, when a sitting president openly supported LGBT movement in America. David Gregory of MSNBC was apt to bring it to the public glare. David Gregory has made a name for himself before he replaced the late Bill Russell of the Florida! Florida! Florida! fame as the anchor man of "Meet the Press". He is skillful with leading questions in interviews and apt to nail, who so-ever is on his interview hot seat.

The response from the Vice President carried his boss views along with it. The President had two options, either denying the Vice President by separating his views from his government which would have been an opportunity for those asking President Obama to drop Vice President Joe Biden for Hillary Clinton who later became the Secretary of State for the VP slot, or flow with it.

The second option was to carry along with the views of his Vice President and explained further the reasons why the Gays or the LGBT movement should be allowed to marry, like the traditional marriage. He took this second option for these reasons as claimed on the America news media.

Some people as well as the conservative press like Fox news believed it was political.

Some including the liberal like MSNBC said the President was convinced and was bringing an evolution

Some mostly the blacks said, the President did not quite consider the political implication of this action.

During President Obama's press interview with Robin Robert of ABC news that followed, he explained the pain of being the commander-in-Chief of those who are receiving the bullets for the preservation of the security of the nation at home and far away countries. He posited that it would be unfair not to consider their feelings and what constitute their happiness. The President was emotional about the plight of the people; the conservative and the evangelical would often call the abominations of the Bible, according to the scripture; but the same scripture asked us to love one another, the President sealed his statement with the golden rule.

The President was asked his opinion on his Vice President's public view of presenting conflicting opinion or jumping ahead of statement which often put the government in public debates. The President replied that Joe Biden is a man who will look at you straight in the eyes and tell you the truth, and that is the kind of Vice President the man with Harvard degree would appreciate, i.e. ability to challenge and bring out the best in him.

Did this challenge or evolution or evolving on the part of the president over state his views on gays? Did the vice President jump the gun before the administration could come out with it or was it a plan to test the water of politics six months before election, knowing the tide of events will soon be watered down and by October it will be about economy not LGBT rights?

Whatever it is the drop in opinion polls for the president and the increase in the polls for Gov. Mitt Romney may be political miscalculations on the part of the President. The bold attempt of the first sitting President to openly embrace the marriage equality of LGBT may be a follow up to the title of his book, "Audacity of Hope" for the gays and those that will demand for more of it in future. Only time will tell.

The Oracle, examined the time the peasants first asked Luis the 16th some questions on equalities, which changed the world of France and the rest of the world, and America's President Abraham Lincoln, who emancipated the slaves in America, until the blood of President Kennedy became the baptism of the freedom and equality of all races in America. Still many groups are asking for opportunity to be who they want to be which to some perceive as a challenge to tradition in the land of opportunities.

Maybe, the President spoke the minds of the majority of Americans on the LGBT right to marry. As the world changes, those still dragging their feet will be left behind as said by President Bush "No child left behind policy". The outcome of the November election will determine if the traditionalists are reducing in number and all the 'conservative values' which may no longer be the values of the coming generation. Therefore, the roles of religion and the traditional values will be determined by the youths, and how they want to see the society they live in years to come.

Professor Babs Fafunwa defined education as freedom from ignorance, and ability to see clearly, just like the scripture demanded for the believers never to stop reading or searching for the truth, likewise, the coming generation, which may no longer consider as important those traditional values, but support those values that will represent the happiness and freedom for their generation. This is the direction the President has taken.

Win or lose, the President has planted a seed that will be difficult to ignore in future as the seven new England States that have recognized same sex marriage may increase to 20 states before 2016 election. The LGBT rights may become the civil rights and if it succeeds, the civil rights may proceed to rights of American Muslims to demand for the same rights like the Christians and other religions. It may be difficult to stop the train of all those that will be cog in the wheel of values and traditions; which may likely take the back seat.

Will the Presidency under Gov. Mitt Romney a Mormon, stop the American Muslims rights if they ask for rights to have more than one wife which is one of the pillars of Islam? Be careful of what you wish for because you may get it. Is this the end of tradition, or is the time to set up a government program to find out why people believe that they are born gays or lesbians and proceed to disabuse these views?. They will always be with us, if we have to co-exist, like others, they must have all the benefits of happiness; this is an issue of concern to the Oracle.

Like the President said, we must be guided by the golden rule "Do unto others what you want people do unto you" meaning do not be selfish with your happiness or your definition of it, not only with marriage but in all things, love and not hate, create room for what makes you to be at peace with every one, like Apostle Paul said in Romans 12:18, if possible be at peace with everyone.

Today, the world population is ten percent LGBT and what can be done to integrate this set of people into the future and find common ground with the coming generation, which may leave the traditionalist gasping. The world is evolving and the programs that keep us together must evolve, with all the checks and balances in place to prevent a breakdown of the moral values of the society.

The task before President Obama is simple, he will roll up his sleeves, convince the Americans of the reason for his open support for the LGBT and if the Americans fail to understand, few months to this election, the president will change his mind, throw the marriage institution back to the

States and allow the Supreme Court to determine if LGBT can marry each other. With this, his election chances for the second term may not be threatened with gays or LGBT right turned to Civil Rights tussle. Only nine members of the Supreme Court will then decide the fate of gay marriage not the Presidency.

The task confronting the United States of America is the revival of her economy, how internet which was a blessing in the nineties is now a monster destroying the job market and how America will tackle this monster in years to come. As the industrial revolution destroyed the agrarian revolution, the internet revolution is destroying industrial market. LGBT rights to marry should not be the major concern of government but how to keep the economy active above all competitions.

The President issued a Presidential Memorandum directing the HHS Secretary to ensure that those hospitals that receive Medicare and Medicaid funds will give gay and lesbian patients and their families the compassion, dignity and respect they deserve in difficult times, as well as widows and widowers with no children, members of religious orders, and others whom otherwise may not have been able to receive visits from good friends and loved ones who are not immediate relatives, or select them to make decisions on their behalf in case of incapacitation.

NINE

∞∞∞∞∞∞∞∞∞∞∞∞∞∞∞∞

SAME SEX MARRIAGE

The embarrassment of a sitting President of the United States of America openly showing support for the same sex marriage has been absolved and the reality of the State controlled marriage institution will take a new dimension in years to come.

The resultant dip in public opinion polls on the presidency has not made any significant impact on President Obama, his support has not changed; among the Hispanics the largest and fast growing group in America is still very intact. The women of all races still have their support for him, the African Americans despite their not too happy posture with LGBT rights, still prefers President Obama - a brother that will be difficult to dump to former Governor Mitt Romney who is after the job of the first Black President in America.

Maybe it was right to have made open the support of LGBT rights and round it up within six months up to the election. After the few weeks of shock, the society is beginning to calm down hoping this election may not be based on the religion or its values, but the economy. The determinant factor will be the performances of both candidates, while those still looking at the birth certificate of President Obama may no longer be talking. My friend who made this issue his focal talk show is no longer enthusiastic about it, and everything appears good for the first Harvard University Editorial President, the man with Chicago Politics who has his team still intact since 2008.

"Let Detroit go bankrupt" in fact let every business from banking to auto industries go bankrupt, if they could not find credit to bail them out" that was the statement from Mitt Romney since 2008. This is the flag bearer of the GOP against the President who stood behind the American workers at a time of gloom and hopelessness for the American economy; during the era of no credit from the banking industry. If the Presidency had not bailed out the economy, the greatest nation on earth would have been paralyzed and reduced to the level of a third world nation. It is on record that President Obama inherited the worst economy in the history of the nation.

No matter what, human memory is always short and limited in capacity; however, the reality of events will never be forgotten. Those who are against the LGBT rights are mindful of their religion, but they have failed to understand that Jesus said "the poor will always be with us" so will the gays, lesbian, and LGBT movement. It is a group that cannot be eradicated, it is indeed the beginning of the end for the traditions that are based on old values which the coming generation may find unpopular and gradually fade away with time.

As time goes on, the rights of each group in the country or any nation may be elevated to civil rights, the Muslims rights on the extended five pillars may be part of the future of Americans, a right that allows them to fulfill the five pillars of their religion which include polygamy. When that time comes it will be the right of their religion to protect the values of their faith, that time may be less than 25 years from now.

Many of the LGBTs are quite sincere and very committed to the progress of the country than those using religion to block the support of the gay's right to marry, which they will rather call civil union because of fear; the word marriage may be corrupted; but really, there is not much difference. The truth is that the civil union or gay marriage has come to stay and the society must learn to live with it. The Oracle like General Collin Powell, has no problem with his marriage.

One by one, the society will be evolving like President Obama in the support of same sex marriage. One of the latest supporter is General Colin Powell, all those that are afraid to support it for political or spiritual reasons openly will be adding their voices and by November 2012 anyone still talking about it will be left behind like "bad habit". This is the truth the Americans and indeed the whole world must learn to embrace.

Readers here should not allow sheer ignorance, omission or commission of their belief system to affect the possibility of seeing a society built on respect for others rights and values. America, as a first world nation has continued to grow stronger in expanding the rights of everyone that lives there. The traditional values based on one religion will be challenged or affected, like the Bible believed and later evolved "Slavery" was never a wrong concept in the past, like women were considered substandard to men, like those who were not Jews were seen as gentiles or "the food meant for children should not be given to the dogs". From the Biblical account, you will observe the Christians values had evolved to accept that slavery was wrong without changing the letter of the new and old testament, like the so called gentiles can be Christians, like you don't even need to be circumcised to be a true believer of Jesus Christ; so it is with all wrong assumptions based on religion will be erased for the rights and freedom of all.

These are the values this article wishes to expand like an unwilling child. Those still hanging to the past will be dragged along or left behind like George Bush "No Child left Behind Policy". This is the future of all societies, not necessarily based on the value system of one religion, but all religions, including that of unbelievers. You may not like it, just hang unto what you believe in a society where others have the same right like you.

Even if it sounds like Sodom and Gomorrah to you, in a world with 7.2 billion people, with only 2 billion Christians and 1.3 billion Muslims, LGBT in whatever name it is called is a term that will always be with us now and for long because that is how it has always been, a life or a world of imperfections.

The future of self-marriage is also coming as the world evolves. What a wonderful world and the key to all these mysteries belong to the Supreme Being, God Almighty HIMSELF.

The current interest rate must be reviewed, if not, America may be indebted to about $20 trillion in 2-3 years as national debt; the future generation cannot afford this.

Zents Sowunmi

TEN

∞∞∞∞∞∞∞∞∞∞∞∞∞∞∞

ECONOMIC NUMBERS

A strong follower of the President Bush policies asked a question that dispensed like a bullet, with the words "how much of sacrifices in terms of benefits will the Americans have to forgo as an individual or group during and after the economic recession to keep the leader of the Free world ahead in the 21st Century?"

The answer to his question is simple and bitter. In a very soul troubling statement "EVERYTHING", from social security, Health care called Obama care, Medicaid, and Medicare, lots of taxes and other fringe benefits, like time and half on overtime that will turn to over dash, and complete reduction in defense spending.

The above, is the picture of the nation at the time President Obama was faced with the most challenging and herculean task of any president of a developed nation. By implication, the country must from now on, cut her coat according to the size of her cloths, not her size any more. This means, the era of long coat is over, no more free money or assistance like grants to other nations. The mess ahead requires sacrifices, it may even lead to the end of trade unions as the power to negotiate will be destroyed, and may result in complete downsizing in everyday life.

Could this be an indication that all the gains of the past or post World War II are over or have been wiped away by the overwhelming 16 trillion dollars debt that started from the hero of the Republicans; late President Ronald Reagan?

The answer to this is terrifying and with the approval to increase borrowing given by the Congress and the Senate, the President had made unwelcome choice for the future generation.

America may have to review its value system, in terms of purchases, from big mansions to what you can afford. The big corporation must help the system to pay tax to reduce the debt, like the Oracle wrote in the past; it is time for the nation to talk to the creditors for a review of the interest rates, which may eventually be the solution to the uncontrollable interest rate on the principal.

The current interest rate must be reviewed, if not, America may be indebted to about $20 trillion in 2-3 years as national debt; the future generation cannot afford this.

After all these, hopefully, will be the glamour of America's prosperity with new value system that will sustain the coming generation. Can the nation afford these interest rates on the national debt?

No president since the time of President Reagan except President Clinton made effort to pay the national debts.

Again, if President Obama loses, it will be because he did not tell Americans in a simple language they can understand how his programs protected the middle class or how his policies saved the country's auto and banking industries, indeed the whole capitalism?

Zents Sowunmi

ELEVEN

∞∞∞∞∞∞∞∞∞∞∞∞∞∞∞∞

UNFRIENDLY ELECTION NUMBERS

Former President Clinton supported some of the attributes of GOP nominee, former Gov. Mitt Romney, including the Bush Tax policy that favors the one percent people in the country: which gradually drained the government of her resources in the last 10 years. Is this a political calculation for President Obama to be a one term President?

What will be the implications for the future of Senator Hillary Clinton in 2016, if Obama is not re-elected in November 2012?

Will America still consider Senator Hillary Clinton for Presidency in 2016, if Obama completes two terms or decides to change Democratic Party from Government, as Americans may still want to preserve the two party structures?

What happens If Governor Mitt Romney's presidency is unable to fix the economy after pulling down all the gains of the Middle class as currently being contemplated; like Obamacare, and some of the benefits won by the Middle class in the last 50 years, can Hillary Clinton be seen as a better candidate in 2016?

Furthermore, if President Obama loses the November elections, it will not be because he did not perform; it will be because America did not give this President the required working tool to succeed. He was given a very hostile GOP led Congress that voted No to all the good programs introduced by a President who inherited the worst economy in the history of the greatest nation on earth.

President Barack Obama, despite his very unique achievements on foreign policy - elimination of imaginary and real enemies of the United States in every part of the world, is still cleaning the economic mess left behind by his predecessor as a result of the unfavorable tax policy that reduced the inflow of funds which technically drained or left the treasury barely empty; the removal of the economic gains of the Clinton years which made the economy operate more like a credit card system.

President Obama is still and will always be seen by conservatives as a stranger in the White House whose birth certificate did not pass the smell test of real qualification for the office of the President of the United States of America.

Chris Matthew of MSNBC the "Hardball" program likened the presidency inherited by President Obama from President Bush in 2008, to a man who bought a house only to find out that the property has been eaten up by termites; the plumbing jobs was an eye sour; many electrical faults; the roofs were leaking and everything seemed to have fallen apart. As he was struggling to fix the property, the children of the sellers were laughing at him and even blocked him from securing a loan to fix the property and later blamed him for not fixing the property on time. Such is the job given to the first Black President which has not been an easy task.

How the President is able to run the economy given the porous tax policy left behind by President Bush is still a wonder. The job creation continues to climb up, though at a snail speed, in spite of lack of cooperation by the GOP controlled Congress to help him improve the economy. With two active wars; and many military locations all over the world; 16 trillion dollars deficit which 60 percent of it could be interests alone; and may increase to $20 trillion in the next four years if the Bush Tax is not abolished, the task is really herculean. Would the country really have to do away with all the social programs to pay off the loan?

As the nation approaches the November elections, the questions the President should be asking the country is what would have happened to the greatness of America, leader of the free world if the "Banking industry was left bankrupt without bailouts" or in the language of Mitt Romney in

2008/2009, "Let Detroit Go Bankrupt", at a time America was losing 750 thousand jobs every month?

What about the 4.8 million new jobs created by this president despite an inherited awful economy which is even more than the total jobs created during the eight years of President Bush who inherited a sound economy from President Clinton?

Again, if President Obama loses, will it be that, he did not tell Americans in a simple language that they can understand how his programs protected the middle class or how his policies saved the country's auto and banking industries, indeed the whole capitalism?

However, he will have to explain how the trust of the economy was demolished before he became the President, a confidence, he had to rebuild without destroying the system or creating fear that would have driven away investors from his country. These are the tasks President Obama confront with every day of his presidency.

What if the ATM cards of all Americans had failed to work in 2009? Would it not have been over for the US economy? This Presidency saved Capitalism which was devastated in the same way Socialism was, during Mikhail Sergeyevich Gorbachev of the old Soviet Union.

History will accord him respect as the President who stood by American workers, the sick, the poor, LGBT, students and immigrants at a time when it was almost over for the country and when Mitt Romney and others stashed their wealth in Cayman Island and Swiss Banks.

The Oracle asked a question, a few weeks ago from all the supporters of GOP to explain the gains or benefits the Republicans provided for the American women, children, the sick, the poor, the students and immigrants in the last 50 years, none, was the answer.

The Party consistently blocked all the benefits of students; it blocked the benefits for the sick, and the poor. It voted against the equal pay for women, the birth control; yet most women from the South and the Evangelicals continue to vote for a Party that stood against the commandment of Jesus in the Parable of the Sheep and the Goat in the book of Matthew 25:31-46 and yet claimed to have more Christians than any group of people in a country with many religions.

2016 will be a straight fight between Vice President Joe Biden and Hillary Clinton for the party nomination, but if President Obama loses in November 2012, Senator Hillary Clinton will be the only choice of the Democrats and the Vice President Joe Bidden will be history.

Could this be the reasons behind the statement and the tactical support of former President Clinton for some of the positive side of Governor Mitt Romney or contributions for the Clinton Foundations to prepare the ground for Hillary Clinton?

The Oracle is just curious!!

The Oracle believes that President Obama will still occupy the White House in the next four years, the President in the last few weeks to the election will be wiser to replay his inaugural speech: how the tough problems he inherited could not be fixed in one term. He will remind the Americans that he was not given a friendly Congress, except for the first two years which made his Obamacare possible. He will say it point blank to the people; he will remind them of the journey so far, on how he cleaned the coastal States when BP oil spillage almost destroyed the lifestyle of about six States.

Furthermore, he will tell the Americans, how Osama bin Laden was terminated, how Muammar Muhammad Abu Minyar al-Gaddafi of Libya was killed in November 2011 and how President Obama's s foreign policy brought more friends to Americans than the hostile environment he inherited in 2008.

The good people of America, the poor, the sick, the workers, the immediate generations of immigrants, the blacks, the Hispanics, the Asians, the women and students will know their true friend and be compassionate with him and give him the 53.3 percent of the electoral votes or more than the 270 electoral college required to keep the Presidency against his rival Mitt Romney as predicted by the ORACLE since August 2011.

If after all these happenings, President Obama still loses, which the Oracle doubts, American Presidents may not be able to have a two term presidency again in the next 20 years as Mitt Romney will be a one term presidency too. When this trend starts, like the Israelites in the wilderness, the Americans will crave for a return to the Obama and Clinton era, that protected their middle class all which would have been weakened by a Mitt Romney Presidency particularly, the Organized Labor Unions which would have been destroyed and the unemployment benefits which would have been cancelled, more people would have turned to crimes, and there would be provision of more jail houses all over the country.

The above scenario is not good for the country, definitely this was not the dream of JFK or LBJ when the Civil rights Bill was signed nor the dreams Andrew Jackson the founder of Democratic Party of America had, which was to protect the sick and the poor within the framework of Capitalism because like Jesus said in the Bible," the sick and poor will always be with you but I will not"

The above, is the reason why President Obama must be re-elected, because he represents the hope of average Americans, particularly, the middle class, who should be protected. Whatever the outcome of the November election, President Obama did more for the American middle class at a time the economy was bad than any of his predecessors; at a time food was to be placed on the table, at a time medicine was needed for the sick, when the insurance coverage was needed for those with pre-existing conditions, when insurance coverage also included those under 26 years, when the student loans interest was reduced. Obama appointed women into Supreme Court; he kept the Presidency of the World Bank in America. It is not how long in office but the positive impact he has made on the people.

Finally, President Obama's place in history is assured, a positive and effective leadership in the time of the worst economic turbulence. Given a friendlier Congress, he could have done better, a President whose shoulder was there to carry the burden of the nation when it was crumbling in 2008. As it is now, with the US economy, the choice is to either give up all the social benefits like Obamacare, Medicare, Social Security to pay off the debts created by Bush as a result of funding of two wars, otherwise make the Rich pay a little more. That would eventually, lead to a yearly income of one trillion dollars required to offset the debt. This is the real controversy between President Obama and the Republicans in November elections, the president is standing on the side of the Middle Class the Republicans through Mitt Romney is standing behind the Rich. Who will blink first?

The greatest challenge to US economy is not the assumed cost of over blown social benefits nor the greedy eyes of the Republicans on tax free policy, it is embedded in the greatest open information technology which used to be the exclusive rights of America but is now available through the Monster called Internet to every nation on the earth, which has eroded all forms of traditional jobs. These are real issues which the next President or the current President will have to confront. The goal of development has advanced for every nation on the earth from physical to intellectual and now to cyber. How can this be controlled and keep America as number one nation is the challenges of the 21st Century.

To restore security to the middle class and create an economy built to last – that creates the jobs of the future and makes things the rest of the world buys -- we have to out-innovate the competition. But to win that competition, American companies must be able to take their ideas market quickly without the constraints of undue regulation and costs. That's why President Obama has directed his Administration to reduce barriers to American business success, including reforming our patent system, reviewing federal regulations, and promoting trade.

TWELVE

∞∞∞∞∞∞∞∞∞∞∞∞∞∞∞

RE-ELECTION BENEFITS

There is no part of the American society that will not be touched by benefits of a second term for President Barack Obama, for example eight crucial benefits have been ascribed to the women alone in thee Affordable Healthcare Act known as Obamacare , annual wellness visit, screening for gestations, testing for papilloma virus HPV, and counseling for sexual transmitted infections, counseling for HIV, contraceptive method and counseling, breast feeding support and supplies and screening and counseling for domestic and interpersonal violence. In addition to this, women equal pay will be enforced, and equal opportunities, on the military, ten goals has been identified from returning heroes and wonder warrior Tax credit with a maximum $2,400 for every short term unemployment and $4,800 for long term and wonder warrior with a maximum credit up to $9,600 per veteran.

Secondly, a challenge to private sector to hire 100,000 unemployed veterans or their spouses by the end of 2013, transition program to the private sector through the Warrior Transition battalion, expand ground forces to meet military readiness, preservation of United States Air Supremacy, with stronger impact and dominance of air, land and sea, missile defense, space and cyberspace and reformation of procurement and acquisition and contractual procedures.

Ω

We are better off today than where

we were as a nation

in 2008, at a time we were

faced with fear, uncertainty

and complete breakdown of

Capitalism and almost the

End of middle class in America.

Ω

President Barack OBAMA

THIRTEEN

∞∞∞∞∞∞∞∞∞∞∞∞∞∞∞∞

ACHIEVEMENTS OF PRESIDENT OBAMA

From the first day in office President Obama worked tirelessly from a collapsed economy he rebuild with over three million new jobs, and some of his notable change and commitment focused more on the women and children

- **Equal Pay for Equal Work**: Signed into law the Lilly Ledbetter Fair Pay Act that ensure women can get paid the same rate as men for the same work.

- **Improving Women's Health**: With effect from 2012 new health insurance plans will be required to cover women's preventive services such as mammograms, domestic violence screenings and contraception without charge.

- **Protecting Women's Right to Choose**: Reverse the Global Gag Rule which banned government aid to international family planning groups. He stood up to the Republicans trying to roll back a woman's right to choose and defund Planned Parenthood.

Still on Health Care, the President passed the landmark Affordable Care Act to restore health care as a basic cornerstone of middle class security in America.

- **Ending Insurance Company Abuse**: Prohibiting insurers from denying coverage to people with preexisting conditions; cancelling coverage when someone gets sick.

- **Keeping Premium Low**: Insurance companies must justify rate hikes; provide rebates if they don't spend at least 80% of consumers' premium on care instead of overhead, marketing and profits.

- **Expanding Access to Care**: 32 million more Americans are able to afford insurance for the first time and nearly all Americans about 95 % of those under the age of 65 will have insurance.

- **Closing the Medicare Prescription Drug "Donut hole"**: Over 2.6 million seniors have saved an average of over $550. Each on their prescription drugs and by 2020, the Medicare "donut hole" will be completely closed.

Some of the promises the President made to address the crises of the middle class produced the following results.

- Job Creation: An economic recovery program supported as many as 3.6 million jobs by cutting taxes, investing in clean energy, roads and bridges, keeping teachers in the classrooms and protecting unemployment benefits

- Saved the auto industry from collapse thereby preventing the loss of more than 1.4 million jobs
- The private sector has created nearly 3 million jobs during the 21 straight months of private sector growth.

President Obama believes American should be able to earn enough to raise a family, send their kids to school, own a home and put enough away to retire.

- **Out-Educating the Rest of the world**: Made college education accessible to hundreds of thousands more students by ending billions of dollars in subsidies to banks and using savings to double funding the Pell grants.
- **Out-Innovating the Rest of the World**: He made substantial investment in clean energy manufacturing

to create the jobs of the future here in America and reduce dependence on foreign oil.

- **Everyone plays by the Same Rule Policy**: He passed Wall Street reforms to protect American families from unfair lending practices, rein in excesses on Wall Street and prevent future financial crises known as "too big to fail policy"

- **Everyone does their Fair Share**: He called for closing tax loopholes to ensure millionaires and billionaires don't pay less in taxes than the middle class.

The last three years of his presidency brought significant improvement and achievement, he kept his word: He brought the war in Iraq to a responsible end and brought home the troops.

- **Committed to Iraq's Security**: The United States of America transitioned full security responsibility to the people of Iraq, and also committed to Iraq's a long-term security.

- **Refocusing on Al-Qaeda** : dismantling the leftover of the group and affiliates, he brought Osama Bin laden to Justice

- **Honoring the Service of Veterans and their families:** The US troops and their families get the help earned and enacting the new tax credits to encourage businesses to hire unemployed and disabled veterans.

Source: www. Barackobama.com

The future is
here already.

FOURTEEN

∞∞∞∞∞∞∞∞∞∞∞∞∞∞∞

WHAT THE FUTURE HOLDS FOR THE TWO PARTIES

Perhaps what started as Republican Democratic Party in the 1790 will in future divide the country on two major lines of political responsibilities; DNC was based on social liberal programs it however evolved from Anti Federalist factions that opposed fiscal policies of Alexander Hamilton as early as 1790. The duo of Thomas Jefferson and James Madison organized the faction that became Democratic –Republican

Party. Their main rival political parties then were Federal Party in 1812 the main reason given for the split was over the choice of James Monroe as President , it was the election of Andrew Jackson that finally cemented the DNC as a political party separate from the joint principles with that of the Republican Party.

By 1830 the DNC had made its choice clear to ally with the common people, it was the first time in American history the poor were invited in the inaugural Ball of the President, and they were allowed to come to the party in their house clothes which made the Republicans uncomfortable. They named President Andrew Jackson "Jack Ass" which later in life became the symbol of the Democratic Party.

By 1850's under the stress of the Fugitive slave law, and Kansas –Nebraska Act and Anti-slavery the Democrats finally left the Party, and under the stress of existing or dwindling partners or members The Republican party emerged

A lot had happened in the history of America political and social commitment to the people and each political party by it actions or inactions had showed it love and respect for the country however, the Republican Party continue to demonstrate the strength of the country without much love for the common people unlike Democratic Party with all the social programs that continue to make the Party a haven for the poor and immigrants, all these has made the Republican membership to continue to shrink almost into complete extinctions and a party that could have look like a true American Party because of the diverse nature of the nation is now looking more like a White color people's Party, and the worst of it they don't seem to care or notice the direction of self-extinction the policies introduce by the party is moving.

Surprisingly, most of the social programs that protects the middle class were introduced by the Democratic Party of America, issues like Social security in 1935, civil rights of 1965, right of women to choose, in Roe Vs. Wade in 1973 in a 7-2 decision by the Supreme Court, Same Sex Marriage rights, minimum wage, and a very conducive environment for immigrants.

As the numbers of first generation of immigrants are increasing from Asians, Africans and Latinos or the Hispanics, the fair on the conservatives and evangelicals are real, the numbers of GOP is shrinking and their policy of non-inclusive is becoming and insensitive to the needs of the future or the general populace in the 21st Century.

The question from the Oracle is simple. What is the future of political parties in America? Precisely, what is the future of the Republican Party in the governance in the United States of America in years to come? The Oracle will predict a complete isolation of the Republican Party in future elections until it can redirect or refocus on the need to protect the middle class the power house of an egalitarian society that separates America from the third world nations, right now, the Party is blind to this reality. The Tea party or the conservative members within the group will drive the party out of power for the next twenty years when the Affordable care Act would have taken a stronger roots into the homes and life of every Americans.

The Party will in future fuse into the Democratic Party to return to where it was in 1790 as Republican-Democratic Party of America, a new party will also emerge out of the left-over of the Republican Party to accommodate the every group of people in America but the name Republican Party and its belief system will be history the only change to this predictions of the Oracle is for the Republican Party to retool and repackage itself as a party that will take care of all, the poor, the sick, immigrant and women even by doing all these it will be nothing but identical twins of DNC which both were in 1790.

What is the role of President Obama and subsequent future DNC Presidents in this direction? The Supreme Court will take a new direction in the second term of President Obama, and most of the social issues like gay marriage, self-marriage, even polygamy will be given attention by the Supreme Court which the Muslim community will demand based on their religion and doctrines of their Holy Books.

Again, the middle class will be protected, the world will be softer to each other, and the greatest challenges will be the internet and cyber war which will continue to threaten America supremacy from China and Russia, a war America will win with the support of all other lovers of peace and freedom in Europe, South and North America, the challenges to America supremacy will continue to be the Islamic world in Africa from the left over of the Sokoto Caliphate, Sudan and East Africa and China which may emerge as the economic base for most nations without civil rights for all its citizens. Finally, the United States of America will open its door more to the Latinos, and discussion will focus on how Mexico will be fused into the Union as time goes.

President Obama and President Bill Clinton will be immortalized as the greatest followers of President Andrew Jackson and both will be celebrated for many decades to come as defenders of the middle class and hope of the future of the greatest country on Earth.

REFERENCES

1. United states Department of Treasury : "National Debt Limit"

2. Goldstein Com Inc. :President Obama photo image /google.com

3. Samuel P Huntington: The Clash of Civilizations: 1997

4. Cary McNeal: 1001 Facts that will scare you. 2010

5. MSNBC: Chris Matthew "Hard Ball" & Morning Joe.

6. White House Press release on writings of President Obama.

7. Wikipedia.org

8. www.BarackObama.com

Zents K. Sowunmi is the President of the Allzents Groups, Inc. Zents holds an MBA and several certifications. He is the author of *Before the Journey Became Home, Cien Maneras De Reir, and* he is also completing work on several other publications.

Zents Sowunmi books are available worldwide. For more information on the author or to purchase autographed copies, please contact the author at Zents@korloki.com.